W9-DCL-229

HD 45.2 .W45 2008

What is the impact of
automation?

DATE DUE

NEW ENGLAND INSTITUTE OF TECHNOLOGY
LIBRARY

At Issue

What Is the Impact of Automation?

Other Books in the At Issue Series:

At Issue

| What Is the
| Impact of Automation?

Roman Espejo, Book Editor

GREENHAVEN PRESS

An imprint of Thomson Gale, a part of The Thomson Corporation

NEW ENGLAND INSTITUTE OF TECHNOLOGY
LIBRARY

THOMSON
—————✳—————™
GALE

Detroit • New York • San Francisco • New Haven, Conn. • Waterville, Maine • London

144317543

Christine Nasso, *Publisher*
Elizabeth Des Chenes, *Managing Editor*

© 2008 The Gale Group.

Star logo is a trademark and Gale and Greenhaven Press are registered trademarks used herein under license.

For more information, contact:
Greenhaven Press
27500 Drake Rd.
Farmington Hills, MI 48331-3535
Or you can visit our Internet site at http://www.gale.com

ALL RIGHTS RESERVED
No part of this work covered by the copyright hereon may be reproduced or used in any form or by any means—graphic, electronic, or mechanical, including photocopying, record-ing, taping, Web distribution, or information storage retrieval systems—without the written permission of the publisher.

Articles in Greenhaven Press anthologies are often edited for length to meet page require-ments. In addition, original titles of these works are changed to clearly present the main thesis and to explicitly indicate the author's opinion. Every effort is made to ensure that Greenhaven Press accurately reflects the original intent of the authors. Every effort has been made to trace the owners of copyrighted material.

LIBRARY OF CONGRESS CATALOGING-IN-PUBLICATION DATA

What is the impact of automation? / Roman Espejo, book editor.
    p. cm. -- (At issue)
Includes bibliographical references and index.
ISBN-13: 978-0-7377-3944-2 (hardcover)
ISBN-13: 978-0-7377-3945-9 (pbk.)
    1. Automation--Economic aspects. 2. Automation--Social aspects. I. Espejo, Roman, 1977-
    HD45.2.W45 2005
    338'.064--dc22

2007034804

ISBN-10: 0-7377-3944-4 (hardcover)
ISBN-10: 0-7377-3945-2 (pbk.)

Printed in the United States of America
10 9 8 7 6 5 4 3 2 1

Contents

Introduction

A t a California State Senate hearing in August 2003, then senator and Internet privacy advocate Debra Bowen asked, "How would you like it if, for instance, one day you realized your underwear was reporting on your whereabouts?" Though it may seem to be the heady, paranoid stuff of sci-fi thrillers and conspiracy theories, such a scenario can become a reality with radio frequency identification (RFID).

RFID is an automatic identification system. It uses (1) a tag (or other device) consisting of a circuit that contains and processes data and controls the transmission of a radio frequency (RF) signal, and (2) an antenna that sends and receives RF signals. If the tag contains a battery, it is an active or semiactive tag. Tags that do not rely on batteries or other external power sources are passive, powered by the small amount of electricity generated in their antennae. Some RFID tags may also be entirely chipless, that is, they might not contain circuits. Technology resembling RFID was employed by the Allied powers for identifying aircraft during World War II and developed for Soviet espionage in the Union of Soviet Socialist Republics (USSR) during the 1940s.

Today, RFID is largely used by manufacturers and retailers to track inventory. The Department of Defense has mandated that its suppliers use RFID tags for shipments. After conducting tests, global retail chain Wal-Mart required its top suppliers to adopt the use of RFID tags in January 2005 to reduce the cost of and help streamline inventory management. The tags have been placed on shipments and merchandise, boosting the efficiency of Wal-Mart's supply chain and deterring shoplifting by tracing the movement of goods in stores. Some libraries use RFID to aid with loaning and tracking books and other materials. Consequently, RFID is anticipated to become an alternative to the bar code.

RFID technology also lends itself to other applications. For instance, RFID tags are currently placed in passports in numerous countries, such as Malaysia, Australia, and in some newly issued American passports. In addition, this technology is currently being employed as a way to collect and make payments at toll booths and mass transit systems in many parts of the world. RFID chips have even been implanted in pets and humans. Technology entrepreneur Amal Graafstra, for example, has one RFID chip implanted in each hand. He uses them, in the place of keys, to unlock the doors to his RFID-enabled home and automobile and to log on to his computer. Graafstra is one of the very first people to have RFID implants, receiving his first in 2005. Such implants have been approved by the U.S. Food and Drug Administration.

The automated and inconspicuous character of RFID technology in storing, receiving, and sending data and tracking movement, however, is precisely why privacy advocates call for its regulation. They contend that RFID tags pose a major threat to consumer privacy because such technology allows retailers unprecedented surveillance and recording of shoppers' activities and movements. Because of the minuscule size of RFID tags, privacy advocates also fear that people may have their personal items unknowingly embedded with them and be secretly monitored by a government, corporation, or other organization. In addition, other critics allege that RFID tags may render individuals more vulnerable to identity theft and that corrupted or altered tags can enable identity counterfeiting. They also argue that the malfunction or breakdown of an RFID system can lead to a serious security breach, especially when such tags are used to gain entry to secured or restricted points of access. Currently the California secretary of state, former senator Bowen suggested at the August 2003 State Senate hearing that "it's not our goal to create legislation that says this technology could never be used. It's to gain a better understanding." In fact, Bowen herself had her pets implanted with RFID chips for identification.

RFID is only one of several technologies within the field of automation. In manufacturing and agriculture, automated processes and robotics simultaneously increase productivity and worker safety but raise the concern of economically displacing human labor and hastening the depletion of natural resources. The desks of health-care administrators and business workers are beginning to resemble so-called "paperless offices" as they make the transition from paper to electronic records. Home automation is being viewed not only as a way to assist homeowners in operating their appliances and easing the burden of chores and home maintenance but as a solution in helping the elderly live more independent and fulfilling lives. *At Issue: What Is the Impact of Automation?* addresses these and other issues that demonstrate the increasing ramifications of technological advancement in an increasingly technological world.

1

What Is Automation?

Thomas B. Sheridan

Thomas B. Sheridan is a robotics expert and professor emeritus of mechanical engineering at Massachusetts Institute of Technology. He is also the author of Telerobotics, Automation, and Human Supervisory Control.

In a contemporary sense, automation can be defined as the use of artificial sensors, computers, and other devices to process data and guide mechanical actions that take the place of human labor. It was first used in manufacturing and appeared during the Industrial Revolution, and now applies to the widespread computerization of automobiles, appliances, electronics, and other devices. Automation, however, is a highly complex and widely misunderstood process, presenting numerous benefits, issues, and problems.

The term *automation* has several definitions. The *Oxford English Dictionary* (second edition, 1989) defines it as follows:

1. Automatic control of the manufacture of a product through a number of successive stages;
2. the application of automatic control to any branch of industry or science;
3. by extension, the use of electronic or mechanical devices to replace human labor

The term's first use is traceable to a 1952 *Scientific American* article.

Thomas B. Sheridan, "Chapter 1: Introduction," *Humans and Automation: System Design and Research Issues*, Hoboken, NJ: John Wiley & Sons, 2002, pp. 9–13. Copyright © 2002 by Thomas B. Sheridan. Reprinted with permission of John Wiley & Sons, Inc.

With regard to the first meaning, in technical writing today the term has easily grown beyond manufacturing, which was the context of the first use. The second meaning is probably the most widely accepted today, but in this case there is a restriction to what is commonly meant by *automatic control.* . . . The third meaning, however, is now gaining wide acceptance—namely, any mechanical or electronic replacement of human labor, where labor is taken to mean either physical labor or mental labor. Physical labor was of concern decades ago; mental labor is of primary importance today, at least in the developed nations. Computers that interpret inputs, record data, make decisions, or generate displays are now regarded as automation, including the sensors that go with them, even though in the strict sense none of these functions may be automatic control.

In the fullest contemporary sense of the term, *automation* refers to (a) the mechanization and integration of the sensing of environmental variables (by artificial sensors); (b) data processing and decision making (by computers); and (c) mechanical action (by motors or devices that apply forces on the environment) or "information action" by communication of processed information to people. . . . It can refer to open-loop operation on the environment or closed-loop control.

The term *computerization* formally refers to the instrumentality (the computer) by which a data-processing function is performed. Insofar as the data-processing function is one that replaces (or could replace) a human, one can say that computerization is automation. . . .

History of Automation

Historically, the first automation was mechanization of manual labor during the Industrial Revolution, although the term was not in use at that time. Steam engines and, later, electric motors were attached to mechanisms that performed routine operations (e.g., sewing, metal stamping) open loop (i.e., without feedback control or self-correction of errors).

Automatic control (feedback control) devices existed early, the most celebrated example being the flyball governor, which was developed to regulate the flow of steam into a steam engine. As the engine shaft rotates faster and faster, centrifugal force acting on the flyballs pushes the balls out, moving against a spring, and making the collar slide axially along the shaft. This motion is attached to the steam entry valve in such a way that as the balls spin faster, the valve closes more, thereby reducing steam flow to the engine and tending to reduce the shaft speed. In this way, with a given setting of the flyball spring, the steam engine comes to an equilibrium speed. Hooking up the flyball device so that faster shaft motion (and flyballs pushing farther out) closes the steam valve is called *negative feedback*. If the attachment were made in the reverse manner, such that faster speed would open the valve, the steam engine would go faster and faster until either it destroyed itself or its speed became limited by its own internal friction.

Another classical example of automatic negative feedback control is the toilet tank. After the toilet is flushed by opening the main valve seat and the water flows into the bowl, the main valve seat then closes by gravity. Then the water supply pressure forces water into the tank and the level rises. As it does so the float ball goes up and eventually forces the supply closure valve down, thereby shutting off further flow into the tank. In this way the water level is regulated to a particular depth in the tank.

Driving a car is another example of negative feedback control, although in this case it is manual rather than automatic. The driver senses whether the car is to the left or to the right of where he or she intends the car to be on the road. If it is to the left, the driver turns a little to the right, and vice versa (this is the negative feedback). In other words, the driver's output—to null any error between desired and actual position on the road—is negative to the visual input. The control gain is the driver's sensitivity to error, the size of the negative steering response relative to the size of the sensed lateral error. The larger the gain, the less the car will deviate owing to any disturbances. . . .

Automation is silent and opaque. It does not reveal its intentions.

The history of automation includes many engineering developments of sensors, actuators, computers, robots, and all the associated physical systems.

The Status of Automation Today

Automation technology has grown sophisticated, driven by market demands as well as theoretical developments that have occurred at a great pace. . . .

Computer chips are now part of automobiles, medical devices, home appliances, cameras, watches . . . the list is endless. All of these could be called "automation" in terms of the third Oxford meaning cited earlier. Automation is now a major part of engineering analysis and design, crossing into every traditional branch of engineering.

A Preview of the Critical Issues of Humans and Automation

In this section some hints are given regarding what humans and automation is all about. The point has already been made that automation is here and will remain. In fact, it has been a kind of technological imperative—design engineers automate because they can—and is not always a good idea.

Humans, too, are here to stay—at least as long as the automation, I hope. The automation is supposed to serve the people, not the other way around. So the two must get along. They must live together. They must work together. They must interact.

Automation is still foreign to most people, though. They don't understand it. The more sophisticated it gets, the less they understand it. When they don't understand it, they may not trust it. Or they may overtrust it, attributing to it intelligence that it really does not have. Automation is silent and opaque. It does not reveal its intentions. The people around it cannot always predict what it is doing at the moment or what it is going to do next.

Automation is mostly stupid and single-minded. Unlike people, it is not robust and adaptable. It does what it is programmed to do, which is not always what is desirable or even what the humans using it or affected by it expect it to do.

However, automation can be made to operate in different ways, provide different displays, be controlled in different modes. The problem is that people forget which display or control mode they set it in. Then they may misinterpret what they think the automation is telling them, or what the automation does in response to their command may differ significantly from what they think they asked it to do.

Automation can be reliable, and when it is, people become bored trying to monitor it. People are really not good monitors, anyway. Sometimes the automation fails, though, and when it does, it may be very difficult for the operator to wake up, figure out what has failed, and take corrective action. There simply may be too little time for the human operator to adjust before serious consequences occur.

One form of automation is the decision aid, the advice giver, the expert system, the management information system. It doesn't act, it just tells people how to act. The myth is that decision aids are always safer than automatic controls because the people can still be depended on. The problem with such systems is that people come to trust them and then to overtrust them. Then the people tend to cease acting independently. At that point the decision aid might as well be connected directly to the machine—the human has no apparent function anymore.

Introducing automation can also be intimidating and alienating. A worker in a manufacturing plant who previously had been a skilled craftsman becomes a button pusher—at least, that's the way he sees himself. He may come to feel that the automation is really in charge, that he has no particular contribution to make, so why should he accept responsibility? The designer of the automation is the only human who is responsible.

It should be evident from these thumbnail expressions that automation poses problems, real and imagined, for the human user or other persons who may be affected.

2

Automation Contributes to Problems of Abundance and Scarcity

Jim Pinto

Jim Pinto is an expert in automation and a technology entrepreneur, writer, and author of Automation Unplugged.

Technologies such as automation create unchecked, problematic abundances. For example, automation has created a food abundance that has led to the rise of obesity because the human body is adapted to store fat and subsist on food scarcity. Furthermore, such technology prospers through creating an abundance of what was previously scarce, eventually undermining its original benefits, such as e-mail's side effect of spam. Artificial restrictions, such as taxation and regulation, are placed on these abundances in an attempt to control them, but such measures are difficult to implement and may not be successful.

Automation has already had a big impact on productivity. Indeed, most of the so-called "jobless recovery" has been caused by the increased effectiveness of automation, which reduces headcount. Offshore outsourcing is responsible for just 15% of recent job losses.

The Problems of Abundance

What do traffic jams, obesity and spam have in common? They are all problems caused by abundance. By achieving abundance, technology destroys the natural checks and balances of scarcity.

Jim Pinto, "The Problems of Scarcity and Abundance," Automation.com. October 2004. www.automation.com/sitepages/pid1698.php. Reproduced by permission.

The technology guru George Gilder has long postulated: "Every economic era is based on a key abundance and a key scarcity." Interestingly enough, many of our current problems are centered on these recurring anomalies. Every new abundance brings its matching scarcities.

The human body was designed to survive on scarcity, and it developed over tens of thousands of years. When food was abundant, it was stored as fat to protect against future scarcity. We are now surrounded by an excess of food, and the body still stores energy as fat for lean days—which no longer arrive. Hence, the obesity epidemic.

The automobile made it possible for humans to travel twenty times faster, reducing natural constraints. When it's so easy to travel independently, everyone does it, and causes traffic jams. The speed and negligible cost of e-mail delivers an abundance of potential customers to anyone with a computer. The huge amount of aggravating spam in your mailbox is a direct result of wide availability of the technology.

When technology creates abundance, it brings problems which are invulnerable to simplistic solutions.

There are lots of other examples. People have always copied music, but in limited quantities because copying an audio tape took time, was relatively expensive and the quality wasn't the same. Today, a CD can be copied easily and cheaply, and the quality is the same no matter how many times it's copied. So, digital music is a cheap commodity—and yet, the music industry continues to expect to sell it as if it were a scarce resource.

Technology has enabled effortless, inexpensive communication with anyone in the world. It also means that sending work to the other side of the world is much easier, and the cost is greatly reduced. Work is now geographically neutral, so almost any white-collar work is being displaced. Joblessness in one place is simply caused by an abundance of equivalent resources elsewhere.

When technology creates abundance, it brings problems which are invulnerable to simplistic solutions. Like genies let loose from the bottle, the new problems are almost impossible to control. Traffic congestion cannot be solved by artificially reducing the speed of traffic, or increasing the cost of driving—through taxation. Obesity cannot be reduced by making food more expensive or less available. Spam cannot be eliminated by making it difficult and costly to send e-mail. The ratios of abundance are too great to be overcome by artificial restrictions.

Any technology which creates abundance poses problems for any process which existed to benefit from scarcity. The beneficial abundances caused by technology usually bring unpleasant societal side-effects. Then we complain about the very things that were previously benefits.

Technology Thrives by Turning Scarcity into Abundance

Think about this: *scarcity=high price, abundance=low price.* New businesses start to provide new alternatives for high-priced scarcities. Indeed, their very existence is to provide goods or services cheaper or faster or better. And proprietary technology advantage brings success—higher margins and profits—which are the very things that business strives for. And patent protection is developed to prevent others from copying, which would minimize the advantage.

As technology advances, competitive offerings become cheaper and faster and better. As competition appears, proprietary advantages dwindle and, unless new benefits are developed, prices and profits quickly decline.

Mainframe computers declined till mini-computers came along, in turn displaced by PCs. PLCs [programmable logic controllers] were expensive and highly profitable till the technology became widely available and they are now cheap commodities. Huge distributed control systems (DCS) were displaced by PC-based software and SCADA [supervisory control and data acquisition] systems. Technology companies must invest heavily and consistently to stay ahead. When they lose their proprietary edge they are left with few alternatives other than service offerings to satisfy their old customer base.

Regulations and Taxes to Restrict Abundance

Abundances continue to expand till the opposing scarcity brings backlash—rules and regulations to artificially restrict the abundance. Perhaps the only way to stop spam is by charging for email. Can food be regulated to stop overeating?

How about tobacco? How much tobacco tax will stop smoking? When it became clear that smoking caused cancer, a warning was required to be printed on every cigarette packet; but that didn't stop smokers. Tobacco companies have paid heavy penalties, which they simply add . . . to the cost of cigarettes, and their stock rides high, bolstered by billions of dollars of "reserves". And today, as part of their penalty, they are required to sponsor advertising that warns about the dangers of smoking, and offers addiction antidotes.

As we get softer and flabbier, there is an abundance of pills, potions, equipment and exercises telling us how to lose weight easily, quickly, safely "in just minutes a day!" Have you seen the proliferation of pill commercials on TV? In spite of tight FDA [Food and Drug Administration] regulations, there are pills for virtually anything and everything. There are some people who actually take several pills, several times a day, without considering possible dangerous reactions. And the pharmaceutical companies manipulate prices through federal regulations.

Artificial Restrictions to Create Scarcity

There are many who manipulate the rules of abundance to cause scarcity. For example, diamonds are found in abundance in nature. But, for over 200 years, the diamond cartel has stifled, by any means necessary, the flow of diamonds from sources not under its control. Today there are synthetic diamonds, with differences that are impossible to distinguish; indeed, they are better than natural diamonds. But the diamond cartel still manipulates the market, to create the "scarcity."

Another major example is oil, once thought to be available in abundance and hence a cheap commodity. But, the owners of abundant resources quickly realized that they could restrict supplies to create artificially inflated prices—the fundamental reason for the existence of OPEC [Organization of Petroleum Exporting Countries]. What will the price of gasoline need to be before traffic is reduced? At what levels of scarcity will alternative energy systems come into play?

The cyclic problems of "scarcity and abundance" are deep rooted in the human condition, in human society. Look around you, and you'll find the causes and effects around you, everywhere.

3

Automation Signals the Robotics Revolution

Marshall Brain

Marshall Brain is the founder of the Web site How Stuff Works and a noted speaker and consultant. He lives in Raleigh, North Carolina.

The growing prevalence of automation in stores, banks, and restaurants signals a technological revolution that will dramatically change the economy, workforce, and our way of life. Just as the airplane and the computer transformed the world within a single century, the automated services of today will give way to the emergence of robotics, and humanoid robots will replace people working in the labor and service industries—as well as numerous clerical professions—within the next several decades. Although this will greatly enhance the general quality of life, millions of people will be economically displaced. Therefore, society must prepare for these changes now and anticipate the economic and social impacts of an automated, robotic workforce.

I went to McDonald's this weekend with the kids. We go to McDonald's to eat about once a week because it is a mile from the house and has an indoor play area. Our normal routine is to walk in to McDonald's, stand in line, order, stand around waiting for the order, sit down, eat and play.

On Sunday, this decades-old routine changed forever. When we walked in to McDonald's, an attractive woman in a

Marshall Brain, "Robotic Nation," *MarshallBrain.com,* 2003. http://marshallbrain.com/ robotic-nation.htm. © Copyright 2003-2004 by Marshall Brain. All rights reserved. Reproduced by permission.

suit greeted us and said, "Are you planning to visit the play area tonight?" The kids screamed, "Yeah!" "McDonald's has a new system that you can use to order your food right in the play area. Would you like to try it?" The kids screamed, "Yeah!"

The woman walks us over to a pair of kiosks in the play area. She starts to show me how the kiosks work and the kids scream, "We want to do it!" So I pull up a chair and the kids stand on it while the (extremely patient) woman in a suit walks the kids through the screens. David ordered his food, Irena ordered her food, I ordered my food. It's a simple system. Then it was time to pay. Interestingly, the kiosk only took cash in the form of bills. So I fed my bills into the machine. Then you take a little plastic number to set on your table and type the number in. The transaction is complete.

We sat down at a table. We put our number in the center of the table and waited. In about 10 seconds the kids screamed, "When is our food going to get here???" I said, "Let's count." In less than two minutes a woman in an apron put a tray with our food on the table, handed us our change, took the plastic number and left.

You know what? It is a nice system. It works. It is much nicer than standing in line. The only improvement I would request is the ability to use a credit card.

Automated systems will proliferate rapidly.

I will make this prediction: by 2008, every meal in every fast food restaurant will be ordered from a kiosk like this, or from a similar system embedded in each table.

As nice as this system is, however, I think that it represents the tip of an iceberg that we do not understand. This iceberg is going to change the American economy in ways that are very hard to imagine.

The Iceberg

The iceberg looks like this. On that same day, I interacted with five different automated systems like the kiosks in McDonald's:

- I got money in the morning from the ATM [automated teller machine].

- I bought gas from an automated pump.

- I bought groceries at BJ's (a warehouse club) using an extremely well-designed self-service checkout line.

- I bought some stuff for the house at Home Depot using their not-as-well-designed-as-BJ's self-service checkout line.

- I bought my food at McDonald's at the kiosk, as described above.

All of these systems are very easy-to-use from a customer standpoint, they are fast, and they lower the cost of doing business and should therefore lead to lower prices. All of that is good, so these automated systems will proliferate rapidly.

The problem is that these systems will also eliminate jobs in massive numbers. In fact, we are about to see a seismic shift in the American workforce. As a nation, we have no way to understand or handle the level of unemployment that we will see in our economy over the next several decades.

Humanoid robots are as inevitable as airplanes.

These kiosks and self-service systems are the beginning of the robotic revolution. When most people think about robots, they think about independent, autonomous, talking robots like the ones we see in science fiction films. C-3PO and R2-D2 [from the *Star Wars* film series] are powerful robotic images that have been around for decades. Robots like these will come into our lives much more quickly than we imagine—self-service checkout systems are the first primitive signs of the trend. Here is one view from the future to show you where we are headed:

> Automated retail systems like ATMs, kiosks and self-service checkout lines marked the beginning of the robotic revolution. Over the course of fifteen years starting in 2001, these systems proliferated and evolved until nearly every retail transaction could be handled in an automated way. Five million jobs in the retail sector were lost as a result of these systems.
>
> The next step was autonomous, humanoid robots. The mechanics of walking were not simple, but Honda had proven that those problems could be solved with the creation of its ASIMO robot at the turn of the century. Sony and other manufacturers followed Honda's lead. Over the course of two decades, engineers refined this hardware and the software controlling it to the point where they could create humanoid bodyforms with the grace and precision of a ballerina or the mass and sheer strength of the Incredible Hulk.
>
> Decades of research and development work on autonomous robotic intelligence finally started to pay off. By 2025, the first machines that could see, hear, move and manipulate objects at a level roughly equivalent to human beings were making their way from research labs into the marketplace. These robots could not "think" creatively like human beings, but that did not matter. Massive AI [artificial intelligence] systems evolved rapidly and allowed machines to perform in ways that seemed very human.
>
> Humanoid robots soon cost less than the average car, and prices kept falling. A typical model had two arms, two legs and the normal human-type sensors like vision, hearing and touch. Power came from small, easily recharged fuel cells. The humanoid form was preferred, as opposed to something odd like R2-D2, because a humanoid shape fit easily

into an environment designed around the human body. A humanoid robot could ride an escalator, climb stairs, drive a car, and so on without any trouble.

Once the humanoid robot became a commodity item, robots began to move in and replace humans in the workplace in a significant way. The first wave of replacement began around 2030, starting with jobs in the fast food industry. Robots also filled janitorial and housekeeping positions in hotels, motels, malls, airports, amusement parks and so on.

The economics of one of these humanoid robots made the decision to buy them almost automatic. In 2030 you could buy a humanoid robot for about $10,000. That robot could clean bathrooms, take out trash, wipe down tables, mop floors, sweep parking lots, mow grass and so on. One robot replaced three six-hour-a-day employees. The owner fired the three employees and in just four months the owner recovered the cost of the robot. The robot would last for many years and would happily work 24 hours a day. The robot also did a far better job—for example, the bathrooms were absolutely spotless. It was impossible to pass up a deal like that, so corporations began buying armies of humanoid robots to replace human employees.

By 2055

The first completely robotic fast food restaurant opened in 2031. It had some rough edges, but by 2035 the rough edges were gone and by 2040 most restaurants were completely robotic. By 2055 the robots were everywhere. The changeover was that fast. It was a startling, amazing transformation and the whole thing happened in only 25 years or so starting in 2030.

In 2055 the nation hit a big milestone—over half of the American workforce was unemployed, and the number was still rising. Nearly every "normal" job that had been filled by a human being in 2001 was filled by a robot instead. At restaurants, robots did all the cooking, cleaning and order taking. At construction sites, robots did everything—Robots poured the concrete, laid brick, built the home's frame, put in the windows and doors, sided the house, roofed it, plumbed it, wired it, hung the drywall, painted it, etc. At the airport, robots flew the planes, sold the tickets, moved the luggage, handled security, kept the building clean and managed air traffic control. At the hospital robots cared for the patients, cooked and delivered the food, cleaned everything and handled many of the administrative tasks. At the mall, stores were stocked, cleaned and clerked by robots. At the amusement park, hundreds of robots ran the rides, cleaned the park and sold the concessions. On the roads, robots drove all the cars and trucks. Companies like Fedex [Federal Express], UPS [United Parcel Service] and the post office had huge numbers of robots instead of people sorting packages, driving trucks and making deliveries.

By 2055 robots had taken over the workplace and there was no turning back.

I know what you are thinking. You are thinking, "This is *impossible*—there will not be humanoid robots in 2055. It is a ridiculous suggestion." But they will be here. Humanoid robots are as inevitable as airplanes.

Imagine this. Imagine that you could travel back in time to the year 1900. Imagine that you stand on a soap box on a city street corner in 1900 and you say to the gathering crowd, "By 1955, people will be flying at supersonic speeds in sleek aircraft and traveling coast to coast in just a few hours." In 1900, it would have been *insane* to suggest that. In 1900, *airplanes did not even exist*. Orville and Wilbur [Wright] did not make the first flight until 1903. The Model T Ford did not appear until 1909.

Yet, by 1947, [test pilot] Chuck Yeager flew the X1 at supersonic speeds. In 1954, the B-52 bomber made its maiden flight. It took only 51 years to go from a rickety wooden airplane flying at 10 mph, to a gigantic aluminum jet-powered Stratofortress carrying 70,000 pounds of bombs halfway around the world at 550 mph. In 1958, Pan Am started non-stop jet flights between New York and Paris in the Boeing 707. In 1969, Americans set foot on the moon. It is unbelievable what engineers and corporations can accomplish in 50 or 60 short years.

There were millions of people in 1900 who believed that humans would never fly. They were completely wrong. However, I don't think *anyone* in 1900 could imagine the B-52 happening in 54 years.

Over the next 55 years, the same thing will happen to us with robots. In the process, the entire employment landscape in America will change. Here is why that will happen.

Moore's Law

You have probably heard about Moore's law. It says that CPU [central processing unit] power doubles every 18 to 24 months or so. History shows Moore's law very clearly. You can see it, for example, by charting the course of Intel microprocessor chips starting with Intel's first single-chip microprocessor in 1971:

- In 1971, Intel released the 4004 microprocessor. It was a 4-bit chip running at 108 kilohertz. It had about 2,300 transistors. By today's standards it was extremely simple, but it was powerful enough to make one of the first electronic calculators possible.

- In 1981, IBM released the first IBM PC [personal computer]. The original PC was based on the Intel 8088 processor. The 8088 ran at 4.7 megahertz (43 times faster clock speed than the 4004) and had nearly 30,000 transistors (10 times more).

- In 1993, Intel released the first Pentium processor. This chip ran at 60 megahertz (13 times faster clock speed than the 8088) and had over three million transistors (10 times more).

- In 2000 the Pentium 4 appeared. It had a clock speed of 1.5 gigahertz (25 times faster clock speed than the Pentium) and it had 42 million transistors (13 times more).

You can see that there are two trends that combine to make computer chips more and more powerful. First there is the increasing clock speed. If you take any chip and double its clock speed, then it can perform twice as many operations per second. Then there is the increasing number of transistors per chip. More transistors let you get more done per clock cycle. For example, with the 8088 processor it took approximately 80 clock cycles to multiply two 16-bit integers together. Today you can multiply two 32-bit floating point numbers every clock cycle. Some chips today even allow you to get more than one floating point operation done per clock cycle.

There are 3.5 million jobs in the fast food industry alone. Many of those will be lost to kiosks.

Taking Moore's law literally, you would expect processor power to increase by a factor of 1,000 every 15 or 20 years. Between 1981 and 2001, that was definitely the case. Clock speed improved by a factor of over 300 during that time, and the number of transistors per chip increased by a factor of 1,400. A processor in 2002 is 10,000 times faster than a processor in 1982 was. This trend has been in place for decades, and there is nothing to indicate that it will slow down any time soon. Scientists and engineers always get around the limitations that threaten Moore's law by developing new technologies. . . .

The computer power we will have in a home machine around 2050 will be utterly amazing. A typical home computer will have processing power and memory capacity that exceeds that of a human brain. What we will have in 2100 is anyone's guess. The power of a million human brains on the desktop? It is impossible to imagine, but not unlikely.

We need to start thinking about that future today. People are talking optimistically about fielding a team of humanoid robotic soccer players able to beat the best human players in 2050. Imagine a team of C-3POs running and kicking as well as or better than the best human soccer stars, but never getting tired or injured. Imagine that same sort of robot taking 50% of America's jobs. . . .

By 2050 or so, it is very likely that over half the jobs in the United States will be held by robots.

The New Employment Landscape

We have no way to understand what is coming or how it will affect us. Keep this fact in mind, the workplace of today is not really that much different from the workplace of 100 years ago. Humans do almost all of the work today, just like they did in 1900. A restaurant today is nearly identical to a restaurant in 1900. An airport, hotel or amusement park today is nearly identical to any airport, hotel or amusement park seen decades ago. Humans do nearly everything today in the workplace, just like they always have. That's because humans, unlike robots, can see, hear and understand language. Robots have never really competed with humans for real jobs because computers have never had the vision systems needed to drive cars, work in restaurants or deliver packages. All that will change very quickly by the middle of the 21st century. As CPU chips and memory systems finally reach parity with the human brain, and then surpass it, robots will be able to perform nearly any normal job that a human performs today. The self-service checkout lines that are springing up everywhere are the first sign of the trend.

The problem, of course, is that all of these robots will eliminate a huge portion of the jobs currently held by human beings. For example, there are 3.5 million jobs in the fast food industry alone. Many of those will be lost to kiosks. Many more will be lost to robots that can flip burgers and clean bathrooms. Eventually they will all be lost. The only people who will still have jobs in the fast food industry will be the senior management team at corporate headquarters.

The same sort of thing will happen in retail stores, hotels, airports, factories, construction sites, delivery companies and so on. All of these jobs will evaporate at approximately the same time, leaving all of those workers unemployed. The Post Office, FedEx and UPS together employed over a million workers in 2002. Once robots can drive the trucks and deliver the packages at a much lower cost than human workers can, those 1,000,000 or so employees will be out on the street. . . .

[T]here will be huge job losses by 2040 or 2050 as robots move into the workplace. For example:

- Nearly every construction job will go to a robot. That's about 6 million jobs lost.

- Nearly every manufacturing job will go to a robot. That's 16 million jobs lost.

- Nearly every transportation job will go to a robot. That's 3 million jobs lost.

- Many wholesale and retail jobs will go to robots. That's at least 15 million lost jobs.

- Nearly every hotel and restaurant job will go to a robot. That's 10 million jobs lost.

If you add that all up, it's over 50 million jobs lost to robots. That is a conservative estimate. By 2050 or so, it is very likely that over half the jobs in the United States will be held by robots.

All the people who are holding jobs like those today will be unemployed.

American society has no way to deal with a situation where half of the workers are unemployed. During the Great Depression at its very worst, 25% of the population was unemployed. In the robotic future, where 50 million jobs are lost, there is the potential for 50% unemployment. The conventional wisdom says that the economy will create 50 million new jobs to absorb all the unemployed people, but that raises two important questions:

- What will those new jobs be? They won't be in manufacturing—robots will hold all the manufacturing jobs. They won't be in the service sector (where most new jobs are now)—robots will work in all the restaurants and retail stores. They won't be in transportation—robots will be driving everything. They won't be in security (robotic police, robotic firefighters), the military (robotic soldiers), entertainment (robotic actors), medicine (robotic doctors, nurses, pharmacists, counselors), construction (robotic construction workers), aviation (robotic pilots, robotic air traffic controllers), office work (robotic receptionist, call centers and managers), research (robotic scientists), education (robotic teachers and computer-based training), programming or engineering (outsourced to India at one-tenth the cost), farming (robotic agricultural machinery), etc. We are assuming that the economy is going to invent an entirely new category of employment that will absorb half of the working population.

- Why isn't the economy creating those new jobs now? Today there are millions of unemployed people. There are also tens of millions of people who would gladly abandon their minimum wage jobs scrubbing toilets, flipping burgers, driving trucks and shelving inventory for something better. This imaginary new category of employment does not hinge on technology—it is going to employ people, after all, in massive numbers—it is going to employ half of today's working population. Why don't we see any evidence of this new category of jobs today?

Labor Equals Money

Right now, a majority of people in America trade their labor for money, and then they use the money to participate in the economy. Our entire society is built around a simple equation: *labor = money*. This equation explains why any new labor-saving technology is disruptive—it threatens a group of people with joblessness and welfare.

Autonomous humanoid robots will take disruption to a whole new level. Once fully autonomous, general-purpose humanoid robots are as easy to buy as an automobile, most people in the economy will not be able to make the *labor = money* trade anymore. They will have no way to earn money, and that means they end up homeless and on welfare.

With that many people on welfare, cost control becomes a big issue. We are already seeing the first signs of it today. The January 20, 2003, issue of *Time* magazine notes the trend

> "Cities have lost patience, concentrating on getting the homeless out of sight. In New York City, where shelter space can't be created fast enough, Mayor Mike Bloomberg has proposed using old cruise ships for housing."

This is not science fiction—this is today's news. What we are talking about here are massive, government-controlled *welfare dormitories* keeping everyone who is unemployed "out of sight". Homelessness is increasing because millions of people are living on the edge. Millions of working adults and families are trying to make a living from millions of low-paying jobs at places like Wal-Mart and McDonald's. Most of those low-paying jobs are about to evaporate. . . .

We are seeing the tip of the iceberg right now, because robotic replacement of human workers in every employment sector is about to accelerate rapidly. Combine that with a powerful trend pushing high-paying IT [information technology] jobs to India. Combine it with the rapid loss of call-center jobs to India. When the first wave of robots and offshore production cut in to the factory workforce in the 20th century, the slack was picked up by service sector jobs. Now we are about to see the combined loss of massive numbers of service-sector jobs, most of the remaining jobs in factories, and many white collar jobs, all at the same time.

When a significant portion of the normal American population is permanently living in government welfare dormitories because of unemployment, what we will have is a third-world nation. These citizens will be imprisoned by unemployment in their own society. If you are an adult in America and you do not have a job, you are flat out of luck. That is how our economy is structured today—you cannot live your life unless you have a job. Many people—perhaps a majority of Americans—will find themselves out of luck in the coming decades.

The arrival of humanoid robots should be a cause for celebration. With the robots doing most of the work, it should be possible for everyone to go on *perpetual vacation*. Instead, robots will displace millions of employees, leaving them unable to find work and therefore destitute. I believe that it is time to start rethinking, our economy and understanding how we will allow people to live their lives in a robotic nation.

4

Expanding Automation Benefits the Economy

Donald A. Vincent

Donald A. Vincent is executive vice president of Robotic Industries Association (RIA), an organization of professionals who work in robotics and automation.

The expansion of automation in manufacturing—particularly the use of robotics—greatly benefits the economy. Robotics today can automate processes with high degrees of flexibility and speed, therefore increasing productivity. Also, robots can be programmed to perform a variety of tasks in automated systems, allowing them to easily accommodate changes in manufacturing processes. Although automated robots may replace some human workers, they largely replace less efficient or less flexible machines. Moreover, expanding automation improves worker productivity and safety, and even creates new job opportunities.

Just how should American manufacturing react to the cheap foreign labor available overseas? Many people have answered this question by proposing tariffs and organizing boycotts, but others are taking a much more productive and proactive approach. More companies in a growing number of industries are recognizing that wealthy societies such as the U.S. have an important advantage—access to advanced technology like robotics.

Today's manufacturers can deploy a generation of robots that have evolved tremendously since Joseph Engelberger and

Donald A. Vincent, "Robots: Flexible Automation for a Strong Economy," *Robotics Online*, February 11, 2005. www.roboticsonline.com/public/articles/archivedetails.cfm?id=1840. Reproduced by permission.

George Devol built the first prototype in 1959. Not only have the precision and accuracy of these robots improved by orders of magnitude but the enabling hardware and software now has the horsepower to perform a wide variety of jobs—from painting cars and tending machinery to populating printed circuit boards and putting pills in packages. The best news about modern robots is that they have evolved to the point where they are readily available and relatively inexpensive. Even the smallest companies have the ability to deploy them with a great deal of success.

Most companies reaping dividends from their investments in robotics have used the automobile industry as a benchmark. Still the largest users of the 137,000 robots already at work in North America (according to 2004 statistics from the industry trade group Robotic Industries Association), the automakers were the first manufacturers to deploy them in their factories. General Motors Corporation's Turnstedt Division plant in Trenton, New Jersey, deployed the first commercially available industrial robot in a die-casting operation in 1961. There, the robot relieved the operator from having to remove hot parts from a die-casting machine producing decorative body hardware. Not only did the operator have to work in a hot, fume-filled environment, but he also had to wear protective gear to shield him from splashes of hot metal.

For the next two decades, subsequent applications at General Motors and elsewhere would focus on relieving people of dangerous, dirty and difficult jobs until the early 1980s, when builders began introducing models using servomotors and microprocessor-based controllers. Although the old hydraulic robots excelled at handling the heavy payloads found in the automobile industry, they were slow compared to conventional automation and cumbersome to program, and often leaked oil. The new servo drives and microprocessor-based controllers introduced during this decade solved these problems and opened the door to many more applications in electronics, food processing, appliance manufacturing, mechanical assembly, and packaging.

A new era began for robotics. Manufacturers began to deploy robots to boost processing speeds and improve quality in a variety of manual and automated applications rather than mainly to relieve workers of dangerous, dirty, and difficult jobs. By the late '80s, a critical mass of robots had gone to work in a variety of industries, which translated to lower robot prices. Because robots could automate jobs that require dexterity and flexibility without demanding a huge investment in dedicated machinery, the number of companies that could afford them grew significantly, which quickly spurred more development.

The expansion of automation is creating new jobs and opportunities.

By the early '90s, the evolution of robots to servo drives and microprocessors had a profound effect on how the robot was used in automated processes. Industry turned its attention to developing tools that would take advantage of the improvements in the robots. Technology like tool changers, machine vision, force feedback, and integrated software application packages allowed the robots to become easier to setup and program, as well as perform more difficult tasks. Consequently, the design of the automated system could use the robot as the centerpiece of the automated process. The focus could now be on: "How much can a single robot do in an automated cell?" The effect was that instead of justifying a robot based on a dangerous, dirty or difficult work, the justification for capital expenditure could now include faster production, flexibility, quality and the automation of tasks that could not be automated using older technology.

What About Workers?

As robots continue to gain greater acceptance and become more widespread, some observers wonder about the welfare of workers. They ask, do robots simply replace low-paid workers and threaten well-paying jobs? The answer is yes and no. Although robots do replace people in some applications, they usually do so in undesirable, risky jobs that are better suited for machines anyway. In most of these cases, the only reason that a person was doing the job in the first place was that other automatic equipment was too expensive and impractical for the task. Because modern robots are flexible and fast, they not only can do these jobs but also have the ability to replace other forms of dedicated or less flexible automation. So, many robots today actually are replacing other machines.

Even though robots sometimes do replace people, one must remember that they also create opportunity. In other words, workers benefit from the fundamental precept of macroeconomics that says that advancing technology is the only way for a people to increase their standard of living in the long run. Advancing technology is the only way to increase productivity (making more, better for less) in a sustainable, desirable, and safe way. In addition, the expansion of automation is creating new jobs and opportunities.

Most labor unions have recognized robots as one of these technologies and have strived to reap some of the benefits. Because these machines have proven that they can improve productivity of workers and give companies flexibility in their production lines to be competitive, unions see them as a means of not only relieving workers of unsafe, undesirable tasks but also protecting their jobs from cheaper labor overseas. So rather than fighting the technology, most unions embraced it, negotiating with management to train their members to operate it.

Promoting Flexible Manufacturing

Given the success in the automobile industry, other industries have followed the automakers' lead and learned many of the same lessons. In labor-intensive jobs, such as populating circuit boards and decorating cookies, robots relieved workers of the tedium and injuries associated with repetitive tasks. Not only did they automate tasks that needed a measure of dexterity and the flexibility to react to change on the fly, but they also could perform the tasks faster and more consistently than people. On production lines already using other forms of automation, they also were able to introduce a measure of flexibility similar to manual operations.

In the food-processing industry, for example, Connecticut-based Pepperidge Farm Inc. began dabbling in robotics in the mid '80s to cure the rising number of repetitive motion injuries among the workers on its cookie lines. Rows and rows of workers along long moving belts had been picking up thousands of cookies all day long for 10 to 20 years, decorating some, making others into filled sandwiches, and sorting and putting all of them into packages. Although demand had grown for the company's products, the volume of any one of them was still too small to pay for the dedicated automation that was available at the time for these tasks.

Robots changed things, however. In them, the company had finally found a form of automation that could accommodate its different, delicate products and various packaging schemes. When the company began installing them on its decorating and packaging lines, its workers' compensation cases fell substantially.

As the production staff gained experience and robotics technology continued to advance, the company began to reap more than just a safer working environment for its employees. It has learned to use the more than 100 robots it bought over the years to enhance productivity and react to market trends competitively.

Not only do the robots perform their jobs much faster than people, but they also let Pepperidge Farm reap some important benefits of flexible automation. For example, at the Milano chocolate-filled cookie line, robotic handling improves product quality by eliminating fingerprints in toppings and reducing other forms of damage to the cookies. The ability to download a new program into the robots is an important part of the company's ability to follow demand. The company can change over its automated production and packaging lines to deliver products in whatever formats its customers want. Wal-Mart, for example, might want fifteen Milano cookies in a special wrapped tray, whereas Target might want ten cookies in another type of package. All Pepperidge needs to do to accommodate a change in buying habits among consumers is to reprogram the robots to put the cookies in a new package.

This ability to accommodate different and changing tastes with little effort is prompting more manufacturers of consumer goods to install robots in their plants. Pressure only continues to mount to deliver products that satisfy changing consumer tastes quickly without having to hold inventories. Because modern robots combine the flexibility previously associated with people and the productivity possible only through automation, more manufacturers are interested in the ability of robots to help their production lines to produce to demand.

Shoes Still Made in the U.S.

In fact, the flexibility of robotics is the reason that Boston-based New Balance Athletic Shoe Inc. can continue to make its running shoes in the U.S., yet be competitive with other brands made in Asia. When robotics technology matured enough for builders of sole molding machines to integrate robots into their products, New Balance bought one of these machines to automate that part of a line that produced its running shoes. The three robots tending the machine reduced the total labor necessary to run it by 31% yet preserved the company's ability to make a mix of sizes economically.

Shoemaking demands a great deal of flexibility because of its complexity. Unlike microwave ovens, for example, each style of shoe must fit a variety of people. Each style has approximately 75 stocking units (the various combinations of different lengths and widths), and each stocking unit comes in a pair to fit both feet. So satisfying demand for the various sizes of any one style requires frequent changeovers, a fact that has made shoemaking a labor-intensive business. Any form of automation must be flexible enough to accommodate the mix of sizes.

With flexible automation, [manufacturers] no longer need long lead times to design processes to make the product, order the equipment, and build the tooling to support it.

Because automating every aspect of the process is still impractical for the lot sizes at New Balance, the shoemaker configured the process for a mixture of people and robots. While the robots perform the repetitive tasks, the people perform those tasks that require judgment, such as checking the quality of the molded soles, adjusting the molding parameters, and making the machine ready to produce different sizes of shoes. On an average day, the machine's operators change three or four pairs of molds so the stations can produce a batch of different-size shoes. Changeovers take about 20 minutes.

A Bright Future

The stories at New Balance and Pepperidge Farm are representative of a trend in the application of robots. Although automobile manufacturing alone still drives 50 to 60 percent of the industrial robot industry, a much more diverse base of users is installing robots into their machinery and processes. And judging by how fast the robot sales are recovering from the last recession, they are eager to do so. In fact, domestic orders in 2004 got off to the fastest start since the record-setting year of 1999, and this strong rebound is expected to continue in 2005.

Feeding this heightened interest is the dramatic fall in the cost to buy, outfit, and maintain robots. Not only have suppliers of robotic equipment been able to amortize their development costs over the years over a growing number of units, but they also have been able to exploit the tremendous, but cheap computing power available today. Consequently, suppliers have been free to encode a great deal of intelligence into their software to simplify programming and diagnostics. Because of the lower purchase price and operating costs, robots now fit comfortably in the budgets of small operations. Intelligence encoded in software running behind the scenes to interpret sensory feedback is also helping robots to cope with new challenges. The advantage of such feedback allows the robot to perform more of the decision-making process based on a visual or force feedback, much as a person would do.

The ability to collect and use this sophisticated feedback not only will reduce the need for expensive fixtures and handling mechanisms to present parts to robots in a known orientation but also will add much needed flexibility in the process. Manufacturers using robots equipped with this technology will be serious contenders in today's—and tomorrow's—global marketplace. They will have a method for designing and delivering new products customized to the tastes of consumers in local markets before demand wanes from changes in customer taste. With flexible automation, they no longer need long lead times to design processes to make the product, order the equipment, and build the tooling to support it. Instead, they can reprogram their robots and begin producing quality products now.

As robotic technology continues to advance, robots will only continue to find their way into an increasing variety of applications. They already have made significant inroads beyond their long-standing applications in the metalworking industries. They are working in the furniture, woodworking, plastics processing, food processing, pharmaceutical, and medical industries. Researchers even are using robots to conduct multiple trials in laboratories, and surgeons are beginning to learn to use them in operating rooms.

These people have taken a proactive approach to the problem of cheap foreign labor. Rather than proposing tariffs and organizing boycotts, they have chosen to reduce their unit costs the smart way: by investing in robotic technology and competing with capital, not wages. Robots give them both the flexibility and dexterity available from people and the repeatability and speed associated with automation. The result is more productivity, the surest and most positive form of sustaining strong profits and remaining competitive.

5

Automation and Advancing Technologies Threaten Labor

Dan Jacoby

Dan Jacoby is a professor in the Interdisciplinary Arts and Sciences program at the University of Washington, Bothell, where he was the Harry Bridges Chair in Labor Studies for 2004–2006.

Technologies such as automation and robotics are becoming increasingly sophisticated and proficient enough to perform complex tasks, threatening the economic survival of skilled and unskilled workers and personal service providers. Thus, labor leaders must help workers compete with automation and robotics by establishing career pathways from low-status to professional positions. Human intelligence and ingenuity are irreplaceable, and the labor movement must help workers capitalize upon these assets. A close partnership between organized labor and educational institutions can help to achieve this goal.

Over the next 50 years, labor's current disagreement on organizing strategies will likely be overshadowed by a darker, more pressing question: "Does society still need people to work?"

To achieve a worthwhile future, labor will need to organize our emerging knowledge-based economy to ensure that the development of human potential is both our principal objective and our main source of employment. There have been many times in the past when analysts have suggested the end

Dan Jacoby, "Labor Pains: The Role of the Worker in a Technological Age," *Seattle Times*, September 4, 2005. http://seattletimes.nwsource.com/html/opinion/2002468141 _sunjacoby04.html. Reproduced by permission of the author.

of work is near. Economists answer that because human wants are unlimited, scarce supplies of goods relative to the potential demand for them ensure employment opportunities.

Yet, without dipping too far into science fiction, we already see the outlines of new technologies that integrate the sensory functions, flexible movements and logical decision-making capacities that have made human beings indispensable in production.

Robots now not only roll on wheels, but they can walk, run and dance (albeit clumsily). Bioengineering has taken on the task of systematically decoding human and animal functions, such as the imitation of muscular systems, to improve machine dexterity. Visual sensors guide automated tasks such as precision welding. At Google and Microsoft, software is being fine-tuned to translate material from one language to another without human intervention.

We must hope that [servants and care providers'] continued survival in competition with automation stems from consumers' desire to maintain human interactions. . .

Much Professional Work Is Vulnerable

Artificial intelligence does not need to be perfected to substantially reduce the demand for human employment in repetitive jobs. Much professional work is likewise vulnerable. For example, the complex knowledge of extremely skilled diamond cutters has been downloaded into decision-making programs and combined with flexible automated tools to reduce human error and increase productivity.

Work on robotically assisted surgery is being funded by defense agencies. Across the country, newspapers have used information-based technologies to reduce labor in typesetting and production. The paper on which this article was printed—

assuming you are not reading it through an electronic medium that requires no delivery drivers—was handled robotically at the printing plant.

It is true that some technology increases the demand for new workers. In colleges and universities, where distance and programmed learning were originally designed to reduce the need for faculty, a whole new line of technicians is now employed to operate, manage and deploy these technologies.

Although technology has not succeeded in eliminating faculty, digital and video lectures that instruct many more students may yet undermine traditional faculty roles. At least for the near term, however, we will continue to need people to design, manage, market and repair these new technologies. These are our knowledge workers.

Even in a knowledge economy, knowledge workers, like industrial workers in the industrial era, do not constitute the majority of employment. At its peak in the 1950s, manufacturing provided employment for over 30 percent of our workers increased productivity and trade have reduced such work to 12 percent today. Employment has shifted to the service sector, only some of which is knowledge-related work.

The roughly 30 percent of the labor force with college degrees typically find themselves in highly remunerated jobs that encourage independence and responsibility. Unionization has made inroads into the well-paid knowledge-based sector by representing increasing numbers of nurses, teachers and engineering occupations.

With a few exceptions, in most other service employment the labor movement is struggling to ensure living wages and decent benefits. Unlike the knowledge sector, personal services such as child care, home care, retailing, security and cleaning are typically low-wage, low-status jobs with little or no security.

The trend toward this type of employment is reminiscent of the upstairs/downstairs economy in which servants and care providers lived in the homes of the benefactors. Unfortunately, even these jobs are potentially threatened in the long run. We must hope that their continued survival in competition with automation stems from consumers' desire to maintain human interactions, and not merely because the wealthy desire to command servants of lesser status.

An Expendable Burden

Employment changes have exacerbated inequality. In 2001, the entire bottom 40 percent of families received only 14 percent of the nation's income, while the top 5 percent took 21 percent. If we don't achieve a better distribution of income, much of our population may be perceived as an expendable burden. That perception can only become more pronounced over the next 40 years as our older-aged population doubles.

While capitalism's periodic propensity to produce economic crises—a failure to put enough income into the hands of those who would buy all the goods we can produce—could yet trigger major reforms, this by itself would not be enough. Labor must produce a better vision of its own for the future.

As machines begin to look more like humans, workers must distinguish themselves through their capacity for human creativity, responsibility, autonomy, and inquiry.

Organized labor's current membership crisis is complicated by job insecurity and changing career patterns. By the age of 36, typical workers have had 10 separate employers. Moreover, fewer than half of workers nearing retirement have 15 years of experience with their current employer. Rapid and continuous knowledge-based innovation undermines job stability. When basic industries cannot provide, workers think long and hard before undertaking the risks of unionization, which include employer firings and strikes.

Visionary labor leaders must enable lower-paid workers to achieve a better share of the nation's wealth by establishing flexible pathways of advancement—or job ladders—across employers. Job ladders provide an opening for conversation between labor, educators and business.

Yet, worker investments in skills and experience are likely to be abused unless agreements are formalized. Only unions can successfully enforce and monitor agreements across multiple employers to secure their workers' upward mobility.

Building-trade unions coordinate multi-employer apprenticeships that give workers the problem-solving skills and independence they need to thrive in the knowledge economy. In New York, the Service Employees International Union provides training that enables members to advance from low-paid home-care aide to professional nurse positions.

Yet, for those consigned to dead-end jobs, such as fast-food servers, no reliable pathways have been organized that facilitate advancement across industries.

Within our children's future, we can expect that technology will continue its successful assault upon labor costs. Still, as technology replaces professionals and personal-service providers, utopians will recognize in this the seeds of success, a time when working people can lay down their spades to live more-fulfilling lives. Yet, the typical worker's capacity to do so depends upon an income sufficient to permit participation in a life of creative activities.

Labor's Challenge for the Future

Labor's challenge for the future consists of ensuring that human development is the primary industry of employment growth. As machines begin to look more like humans, workers must distinguish themselves through their capacity for human creativity, responsibility, autonomy and inquiry.

Often unnoticed in labor circles is the indirect competition it faces from the rise of a university system that is widely regarded as the guardian of economic opportunity in the U.S. Universities fuel the economy with trained labor, basic research and direct employment. They do so in a way that generally leaves their students in blissful ignorance of, or even hostile to the legacy of labor and class conflict.

Armed with degrees and youthful optimism, it frequently takes graduates years before they realize that protections blue-collar workers achieved through struggle are not theirs. This is no accident: The fantastic rise of modern education has been, in part, motivated by the desire to insulate employers from worker control over the supply of skill.

Innovation creates wealth by discarding old ways and products in favor of more efficient and effective practices. Successful entrepreneurs who seize new opportunities enrich themselves and much of society, but capitalism does not require these winners to compensate the losers. As knowledge, human capital and innovation increase in importance, labor must find a way to tax successful innovation and repair the lives change has disrupted.

Rather than an industrial strategy, it is time to pursue a strategy in which labor partners with knowledge creators to make the university the center of industry and community. Knowledge work in the university is salaried, not driven by profits. The university creates an alternative space to ensure that investments in knowledge are not privatized to benefit only the few. Many will fear commercialization of academia, but the university has always sold its products and has not yet undermined its distinctive commitments to tradition, discipline and science.

A transformation of basic societal institutions such as this is not unprecedented. The family unit once dominated our economy in the way that industry does today, and in an earlier period, religion did much the same thing. Academia's integration into our economy and community is already substantial. Yet, clearly, higher education is not without its own problems.

Organized labor can add to the university by bargaining how students are prepared for work (and life), how workers are treated in their university jobs and, most importantly, how university knowledge contributes to the larger economy.

Together, labor and academia can strive for a world that encourages continuous human development through work and study spanning the seams of knowledge that separate the arts, professions and science. The vision of uniting labor with the knowledge sector seems more attractive, and likely more sustainable, than alternatives that rely upon labor's partnership in systems predicated exclusively upon greed or power.

6

Automation Threatens Manufacturing Jobs More than Outsourcing

Wes Iversen

Wes Iversen is managing editor at Automation World, *a magazine for automation professionals.*

Productivity increases due to automation—not the outsourcing of labor overseas—account for manufacturing job losses in the United States. In fact, China, which is often singled out as being the culprit for American factory job losses, is experiencing a decline in manufacturing jobs because of automation. Likewise, manufacturing job growth in India has remained flat even though its economy is thriving. These trends will continue, as manufacturers must constantly invest in automation and other innovations to maintain productivity.

For many Americans, the word "outsourcing" conjures up images of manufacturing job decline. But the United States is far from alone in losing manufacturing employment, points out Dan Miklovic, vice president and research director at GartnerG2, the business research arm of Stamford, Conn.-based Gartner Inc. "Recent studies show that manufacturing jobs are declining everywhere," said Miklovic, during a Nov. 17 [2003] panel discussion on outsourcing, part of a Global Media Summit sponsored by Rockwell Automation, Milwaukee.

Wes Iversen, "Outsourcing Not the Culprit in Manufacturing Job Loss," *Automation World*, December 9, 2003. www.automationworld.com/view-320. Reproduced by permission.

Over the past decade, U.S. manufacturing jobs have declined by more than 11 percent, Miklovic noted. But at the same time, Japan's manufacturing employment base has dropped by 16 percent, while the number of manufacturing jobs in countries including Brazil have declined by some 20 percent, he pointed out. "And one of the largest losers of manufacturing jobs has been China," Miklovic added. "We like to pick on China and say that all of these jobs are going to China, but they're losing jobs in manufacturing as well."

The reason for the job losses? Miklovic summed it up in one word: automation. Through automation, he said, "we are really doing a good job of improving the productivity of people."

Miklovic reminded media attendees at the panel session that 25 percent to 30 percent of the U.S. population was at one time involved in agricultural jobs. But today, only 3 percent of Americans work in agriculture, yet they have turned the United States into a net agricultural exporter, he noted. "The same thing is now happening in manufacturing," Miklovic said. "Through automation, through improved productivity, we're driving the number of jobs down on a global basis."

Job Loss in India

Confirmation came from another panel participant, K. Muralidharan, senior general manager for Sundram Fasteners Ltd., a major Indian automotive parts manufacturer. In India, he said, growing use of automation is holding down manufacturing job growth despite the large amount of outsourcing work that is flowing to the country. "I find that outsourcing in India has actually cost jobs in Indian industry, though in the long term, it will probably have a positive effect on employment," Muralidharan said.

Manufacturing employment remains at about the same level in India today as it was during the recession of the late

1990s, according to Muralidharan. "The Indian economy is booming now, and it is predicted that in the next five years, the curve will only be upward. But still, the jobs and employment are not really growing at the same pace," said Muralidharan. "The economies of scale that have been created due to outsourcing from developed countries have forced Indian industry to take on automation heavily, which was not the case about 10 years back," he said.

GartnerG2's Miklovic noted that the use of automation contributes to a cyclical situation in many industries. When a U.S. manufacturer develops a new product, for example, the company has first-mover advantage for a time. But in the next phase, when other manufacturers enter the market, competition often shifts to price. In response, some U.S. producers may move manufacturing offshore to developing nations, to take advantage of lower labor costs. However, said Miklovic, they frequently find that the level of automation and technology available in developing nations is less than that of the United States.

A Lesson for Manufacturers

This means that U.S. manufacturers who then invest in sophisticated automation technology at home can gain the upper hand for a time over lower-priced imports, thanks to the higher quality product allowed by the automation, said Miklovic. But the automation technology used in the developing nations eventually catches up, giving products produced there the advantage, he added.

"We see this in semiconductors all the time," Miklovic said. "Semiconductors typically have been produced in Japan and Taiwan. But now there is a booming semiconductor market that's starting in China." While the density and sophistication of semiconductor chips produced in China cannot yet match that of Japan and Taiwan, said Miklovic, China's technology is moving in that direction.

"Automation only works for a period of time," said Miklovic. The lesson for manufacturers is that they must continually reinvest in automation and innovation, he said. "If you stand still, ultimately you lose."

Automation Benefits Agriculture

John K. Schueller is a professor at the Department of Mechanical Engineering and the Department of Agricultural and Biological Engineering at the University of Florida, Gainesville.

As mechanization profoundly transformed agriculture in the twentieth century, the automation of modern farming systems helps today's farmers and workers to continue to produce an abundance of food. Despite the fear that expanding automation will decimate farming jobs, studies demonstrate that it has increased the use of paid labor and that the American economy absorbs workers displaced by automation. To meet current and future agricultural challenges, farms will rely not only on automation, but on innovations in electrical engineering, computerization, and biotechnology.

"The majority of all men who have ever lived have been bound to drudgery on the land. We are breaking away from that servitude." So begins a 1960 book on agricultural mechanization. At the start of the 20th century a U.S. farmer fed about 2½ people. Today, that farmer feeds 97 Americans and 32 living abroad. This revolution has released the rest of the population to pursue the intellectual, cultural, and social development that has resulted in our modern society. Agricultural mechanization, like manufacturing, can be viewed

John K. Schueller, "In the Service of Abundance," *Mechanical Engineering*, vol. 122, no. 8, August, 2000, pp. 58–65. www.memagazine.org/backissues/membersonly/aug00/features/service/service.html. © 2000 Mechanical Engineering magazine (the American Society of Mechanical Engineers International). Reproduced by permission.

as an enabling technology that made possible the other advances of the 20th century.

Many innovations in agricultural mechanization occurred in the middle of the 19th century. Cyrus McCormick's reaper and the thresher first appeared in the 1830s. The steam engine and the steam plow were developed before the American Civil War. But, as Abraham Lincoln said about the steam plow, "To be successful, it must, all things considered, plow better than can be done by animal power." The value of horses and mules on American farms exceeded the worth of all the machines and equipment, including the animal-powered equipment, past 1910. It took the further developments and engineering of the 20th century to make agricultural mechanization a success.

The Tractor's Pull

Agricultural mechanization is often exemplified by the development of the tractor. By 1900, about 5,000 traction engines were being produced by 30 companies every year. These giants, operating at steam pressures of 150 to 200 pounds per square inch, often weighed more than 20 tons. But universal adoption of mechanical power depended upon the internal combustion engine, which was being applied to tractors and other uses at that time.

A key figure in the development of tractors was a Michigan farm boy who first became interested in technology when he saw a large steam traction engine. He started experimenting in 1900 and developed an experimental tractor in 1907. But Henry Ford suspended his tractor work to develop and produce the Model T. Finally, in 1916 the Fordson tractor was introduced. Being lightweight, mass-produced, and low-cost, it was a fierce competitor to the other tractors of its time. It eventually achieved 75 percent market share in the United States and 50 percent worldwide.

Some agricultural innovations are adopted quickly. For example, the FMC [Ford Motor Company] mobile green pea harvester/sheller was essentially adopted in three years in the late 1950s because of its obvious superiority over stationary shellers. But the tractor is a universal tool used in widely differing regions, crops, and farms. The adoption rate varied, depending upon crop prices, the economy, and labor availability. For example, the Fordson was helped greatly by the labor shortage of World War I. But the number of tractors on U.S. farms showed a substantial upward trend for 50 years, starting in 1915. A peak production of virtually 800,000 was reached in 1951. Now that the United States is fully tractorized, about 100,000 are sold annually.

Some current commentators anticipate the complete automation of farms within the next couple of decades. They see dire consequences in unemployed labor. But empirical data might contradict this pessimism.

The adoption of the gasoline tractor was aided significantly by successful demonstrations and tests. The 1908 public demonstrations in Winnipeg [in Manitoba, Canada] were particularly significant. Nebraska passed a tractor test law in 1919. Rather than hurting sales, the compulsory testing verified the manufacturers' claims and showed the potential of certain models.

The tractor was continually refined during the rest of the 20th century to be more efficient, productive, and user-friendly. Contemporary tractors perform four times the work per gallon of fuel as the first Nebraska test subjects. The development of the nimble general-purpose tractor in the mid-1920s, led by International Harvester's Farmall model, made horses completely obsolete, even for small jobs.

Unfortunately, the early tractors were not just user-unfriendly, they were harmful and dangerous. Older farmers' hearing test results often show a distinctive notch around 4 kilohertz. The seats often amplified the accelerations of the rough terrain at the spine-damaging frequencies. Worst of all, many farmers lost their lives in tractor overturns. Today's farmers are much safer if they wear their seat belts and follow proper operating procedures.

One example of the several areas in which the needs of tractor productivity, efficiency, and user-friendliness come together is the power transmission from the high-speed engine to the low-speed wheels. Conventional gear transmissions, somewhat similar to automobile manual transmissions, continue to be used. However, they may have as many as 44 speeds. In the late 1950s and early 1960s, on-the-go shifting without operator clutching became commercialized

Infinitely variable hydrostatic transmissions soon followed, but their commercial popularity has been limited to harvesting machines and special-purpose tractors where the reduced efficiency can be tolerated. Hydromechanical transmissions appeared in the late 1990s to provide infinite speeds at higher efficiencies. The farmer now easily selects the travel speed for the best productivity, and the engine and transmission provide that speed at peak efficiency.

Tractors are expected to provide propulsion power across soft soils. Traction is frequently the limiting factor in performing a job. At the beginning of the 20th century, large steel wheels were used. Now a debate rages between large radial tires and rubber belt tracks.

There has been a substantial increase in tractor travel speeds, which has had a significant effect on the other equipment. Planters, tillage equipment, and other machinery must now perform satisfactorily at those speeds and their controllers must have sufficient dynamic response.

Reaping What's Sown

The many 20th-century advancements in machinery to till soil, plant, remove weeds, and apply fertilizers and pesticides are too numerous to discuss here. But at least harvesting equipment should be discussed because its mechanization trailed only tractors in importance.

Cyrus McCormick's reaper replaced human-powered cutting tools in small grains with a horse-drawn machine in the 19th century. During the 20th century, the rest of the operations, including threshing and separation, were blended into the modern "combine." The productivity gains from many improvements have advanced grain harvesting from 10 kilograms per man-hour to as high as 60,000 kg/man-hour today. The importance of these machines can be seen by the special World War II approval for Massy-Harris to build 500 combines to follow the ripening small grain crop from Texas to Canada in the Harvest Brigade.

The mechanization of harvesting other crops was also important. The corn picker was developed in the early 1900s and the hay baler in the 1930s. After much expense and effort, cotton harvesting was mechanized in the 1940s. But innovations continued to improve the productivity and quality of the job performed throughout the century. The heavy, summer labor of manually handling small rectangular bales was relieved by the development, in the 1970s, of the baler, which produces the large, cylindrical hay bales that now commonly dot the countryside.

Automation of the Field

Agricultural mechanization developments early in the 20th century were spurred by new restrictions limiting immigrants into the United States. A contemporary question is what will happen to those U.S. fruit and vegetable crops for which manual harvesting constitutes more than half the total labor requirement. Most harvesters of some commodities are illegal entrants to the country because the work is seasonal, rural, and unappealing to most U.S. residents.

Perhaps the future is indicated by the trend in tomatoes. The tomatoes processed for pastes and sauces are mechanically harvested. Fragile, fresh-market tomatoes are moving to Mexico, accelerated by the North American Free Trade Agreement.

Agricultural mechanization has always been a political-social issue. Increasing farm consolidation has made many farmers and farm employees redundant, and has decimated some rural towns. Some current commentators anticipate the complete automation of farms within the next couple of decades. They see dire consequences in unemployed labor.

But empirical data might contradict this pessimism. The U.S. economy has absorbed the labor released over the last century to generate a high standard of living. India is another, very different, demonstration. It is the world's largest tractor producer and consumer, with almost 280,000 predicted for this year. Indian farmers feed almost one billion people (although a large number of them poorly) and export grain. Compare their situation to the few countries in Africa with more than 80 percent of the agricultural energy supplied by humans, and their problems with inadequate food supply.

While seed genetics, agronomic practices, and political stability are rightly credited, the contribution of appropriate agricultural mechanization to food security should not be forgotten. A detailed study of paired Indian villages found that the tractorized villages were able to produce more crops per year by having the needed power at critical times. Not only was the production increased, but so was hired labor use.

Mechanization has reduced labor in the developed countries, but has not eliminated it. A very popular attraction at the big Century of Progress Fair in Chicago in 1933 was the radio-controlled tractor. However, its unmanned successors have not found commercial success.

But automation has had many achievements in improving machine performance. The self-leveling combine was an early example. Perhaps the most famous was the ingenious system patented by Harry S. Ferguson to control the depth of implements in the soil. Its hydromechanical servo kept a constant load on the tractor. His 1939 oral agreement with Henry Ford allowed Ford, who had left tractor manufacturing, to reclaim much of his lost market share. Unfortunately, the collaboration ended in a nasty and record-breaking lawsuit.

The last third of the 20th century was dominated by electronics automation rather than mechanical and hydromechanical. Bob Dickey and Jack Littlejohn formed DICKEY-john Corp. to manufacture a monitor to verify that individual seeds are being planted correctly. Subsequently, an entire agricultural electronics industry has developed to the extent that there is now difficulty in standardizing electronic communications among the many sensors, controllers, and actuators.

Power on the Farm

The inclusion of electronics brought the mechanical and agricultural engineers who dominated agricultural mechanization into contact with electrical engineers at the end of the century. But that was not the first time. An argument can be made that stationary farmstead mechanization was just as important as tractors and other mobile equipment. This was achieved during the 20th century by electrification of the barns, sheds, granaries, and greenhouses.

The first use of electricity was in the farmhouse, raising the rural standard of living. Electrification eased the burden of farm women who shared their urban sisters' household workload in addition to often-unrecognized farm duties. But soon lights were also on in henhouses, increasing egg production. A study in Wisconsin showed that good farmstead lighting saved an hour per day by making work more productive.

One of the innovations aided by electrification was the milking machine. Imagine the labor that would be required to hand milk the thousands of cows in some contemporary herds. Gustav de Laval, famous for his 92 Swedish patents and 37 founded companies, was a key contributor to the milking machine. However, despite also inventing the centrifugal separator and the steam turbine and being a Ph.D. in engineering, he died in poverty.

The area of the greatest contemporary excitement and growth is what goes by the poorly chosen term of 'precision agriculture.'

Even in 1919, only 1.9 percent of U.S. farms had electric power. By 1960, the coverage had increased to 97 percent. The peak effort came in 1949, when 707 miles of power lines were constructed every workday. Some greatly credit President [Franklin] Roosevelt's 1935 executive order establishing the Rural Electrification Administration. Other political views say that electrification was already inevitable.

The first known farm installation of an electric motor was on an irrigation pump in 1898. At the start of the 20th century, irrigation was practiced on 16 million acres. Four times that amount of land is now irrigated using electric and internal combustion motors to drive pumps, with less dependence on gravity flow. Water and energy-use efficiencies have been increased by the development of various technologies using tubes, pipes, and low pressure.

The green circles in America's heartland make center pivot irrigation technology vividly apparent. Frank Zybach sold his patent for the center pivot to Valmont in 1953. With one end of a pipe located at a well or other water source, the long pipe travels on wheels applying water, fertilizer, and pesticides around the circle.

Electricity at the farmstead has also permitted environmental controls for barns and greenhouses. These controls, developed throughout the century starting from simple fans, encourage peak productivity from animals and plants. For example, temperature, humidity, solar radiation, and artificially elevated CO_2 can be optimized for production of a specific vegetable.

With the mechanization of harvesting, a similar mechanization of storage and the processing of harvested crops was required in order to handle the huge volumes quickly. Engineers have developed sophisticated, productive systems for such operations as drying, cooling, and storage. Their tasks were greatly complicated by the fragility and quality-maintenance demands of some commodities.

Indeed, the whole processing and food engineering area could be viewed as a significant innovation of the 20th century. The 19th-century consumer had primarily local, in-season foods. Now all foods are always available, through canning, freezing, or refrigerated transportation.

All of the above achievements, and many more, depended heavily upon engineers in the 20th century. Although some technologies had their roots in the 19th century, it was not until the 20th that they were refined enough to be commercially successful. Mechanical engineers joined farmers and craftsmen with mechanical aptitude to perform the work that led to successful mechanization.

Future in the Present

It is difficult to predict the future. In 1960, a top tractor expert predicted nuclear or electric-powered tractors. Even his short-term prediction of higher-octane engines was wrong, as the industry immediately converted to diesel. However, extrapolations from the present remain the most reliable prediction method.

The area of the greatest contemporary excitement and growth is what goes by the poorly chosen term of "precision agriculture." Mechanization has caused farmers to lose their ability to treat each animal or small area within a field individually. The record-keeping capability of computers allows that ability to be recovered.

Precision agriculture essentially came to animal agriculture in the 1960s. Computerized records of milk production and animal physical characteristics were used to select artificial insemination for individual cows to improve the next generation. Transponders were introduced in 1968 so each cow could receive the optimum feed from feeding machines.

Precision agriculture for plant agriculture started in the 1980s, but is just now receiving widespread commercial acceptance Soil-Teq (which is now owned by AgChem) developed a fertilizer and pesticide applicator that changes rates on the go according to predetermined maps. A team of Texas A&M University engineers, including this author, developed a system that automatically generated maps of the crop yield during harvest. Contemporary precision agriculture uses the global positioning system and geographic information systems to manage each small area within a field.

An example of the future is what we envision for the almost 100 million citrus trees in Florida.

Databases will include historical records of production, soil parameters, tree characteristics, and pests for each tree. The water, fertilizer, and pesticide to each tree will be controlled to maximize economic returns. This procedure would also serve to prevent the overconsumption of water and the excess introduction of chemicals into the environment. Many of the component technologies are currently being tested or are seeing limited commercial adoption.

Accurate sensing in the heterogeneous physical/chemical/ biological environments of agriculture is difficult. Accurate control of actuators is also not trivial. For example, imagine mixing and accurately applying granular and liquid materials to many small areas with a 20-meter-wide applicator traveling 30 kilometers per hour.

All other areas of the agricultural industry also require substantial engineering efforts. For example, the possibility of replacing large tractors, which can compact the soil, with small, lightweight robots can't be effectively evaluated until such robots are designed. As another example, harvesting and processing equipment is needed for the new pharmaceutical crops developed through biotechnology.

Taking a Biological Tilt

Unfortunately, there has been little applied research and development in such areas. The National Science Foundation and other engineering supporters leave the area to the U.S. Department of Agriculture and the land-grant universities. But they are taking a biological tilt, especially to biotechnology. Due to the maturation of the market and the low agricultural-crop prices affecting farmers' purchasing power, the agricultural equipment industry has retrenched and consolidated.

Although there were 186 tractor manufacturers in 1921, there are now only two U.S. corporations, Deere and AGCO, producing a substantial number of tractors. In addition, Fiat-controlled CNH [Case New Holland], which includes the remnants of International Harvester and Ford, has a substantial presence.

Perhaps their engineers, and those from companies that make the other types of agricultural equipment, will continue the tradition of improving agricultural mechanization to increase productivity, efficiency, product quality, and environmental protection. Ample amounts of good food will continue to be mankind's primary need as the world's population and its desired standard of living continue to increase.

8

Traditional Farming Should Not Be Overlooked

John Ikerd

John Ikerd is professor emeritus at the College of Agriculture, Food, and Natural Resources at the University of Missouri, Columbia. He is also the author of Sustainable Capitalism: A Matter of Common Sense.

Agricultural technologies, such as automation, mechanization, and computerization, and the aim to maximize productivity have overshadowed the vital importance of traditional farming. The latter emphasizes sustainability and treating farmlands as living, renewable systems, not resources to exploit for profit. Consequently, relying solely on technological innovations has dire consequences—industrialized corporate farming operates without the environmental wisdom farmers and small farms use to cultivate their crops, depleting natural resources without regenerating them. As these resources continue to dwindle, American agriculture must adopt the principles of traditional farming and not replace human ingenuity and productivity with agricultural technologies.

American agriculture seems almost obsessed with endless innovation. Technologies of the past have made it possible for fewer farmers to provide Americans with a vast array of high-quality foods at affordable prices, we are told, and new biological and electronic technologies seem destined to

John Ikerd, "Innovation Through Tradition for Small Farm Success." Presented at the 2005 California Small Farm Conference, "Traditions and Innovation in a Changing World," Ventura, CA, November 13–15, 2005. http://web.missouri.edu/˜ikerdj//papers/ Ventura-SF-trad-innov.htm. Reproduced by permission of the author.

revolutionize American agriculture in the future. Biotechnology is proclaimed as the solution to world hunger and the savior of the natural environment. New electronics will allow us to trace foods back to their farm and field of origin, leading to dramatic improvements in food safety and food quality. New management systems guided by electronics will support new global food supply chains, ensuring the widest possible variety of foods for all at the lowest possible cost, so we are told. But, where is the farmer in all of this innovation?

As the importance of off-farm technologies has grown, the importance of the farmer has been diminished. That's why U.S. agriculture today supports only a third as many farmers as in the 1930s and why 90% of the income of farm families today comes from off-farm employment. Why should farmers expect [to] make a living farming when the developers of technologies are doing the economically important things? Those who have done the thinking, meaning those who developed the technologies, have also received the benefits. And, if future advances in agriculture come from new off-farm technologies, rather than on-farm thinking, the role of the farmer will be diminished still further in the years ahead.

If the new agricultural technologies fail, as all industrial *technologies ultimately will, the future of human civilization will depend on innovative, thinking, caring farmers.*

But, do we really believe we can meet the challenges of a growing world population and dwindling resources with still more new technologies? If not, or even if we are just not sure, we shouldn't be treating farmers as if they are intellectually obsolete. We should be encouraging innovations that enhance the ability of farmers to use their inherently human capacities of ingenuity, imagination, and creativity to address the challenges of the future. Why should we risk leaving all of the thinking to a few scientists in corporate laboratories when we still have a couple of million farmers who are perfectly capable of thinking as well? If the new agricultural technologies fail, as all *industrial* technologies ultimately will, the future of human civilization will depend on innovative, thinking, caring farmers.

Agriculture

Historically, agriculture was not nearly as much about innovation as about tradition. Traditions are made up of "beliefs, opinions, customs, and stories that are handed down from one generation to the next . . . by word of mouth or by example." Traditions make up the cultural half of agri*culture*, "the integrated patterns of human behavior, including thought, speech, action, and history, which depend upon the uniquely human capacity for learning and transmitting knowledge from one generation to another." Culture and traditions go beyond the things people do to be productive or to earn a living, beyond their individual material well-being, to include all of those things that connect us to each other and connect people across generations.

Both the challenges and the opportunities confronting American farmers today, particularly those on small farms, are a direct consequence of the abandonment of time-honored agricultural traditions. Small farmers who rely on technological innovations to bring them into the mainstream of industrial agriculture are destined for disappointment. On the other hand, those who innovate by returning to traditional agrarian values, by restoring culture to agriculture, will find a growing number of like-minded consumers who are willing to help them create a new, sustainable agricultural mainstream. The key to small farm success in a changing world is innovation, but not through biotechnology, electronic sensors, or becoming part of corporate supply chains. The key to small farm success instead is innovations linked to traditional agri*cultural* values. Farmers of the future will succeed by using their uniquely human capacities to care for the land, care for their neighbors, and care for their customers and for people in general, in an increasingly uncaring world.

The promises of new biological and electronic technologies are empty because they are but the latest new tools of an out-of-date industrial approach to farming, epitomized by new global food supply chains. An industrial agriculture is fundamentally incapable of meeting challenges of dwindling resources in an increasingly crowded world. An industrial agriculture quite simply is not sustainable. The industrial paradigm of development is inherently extractive and exploitative, and thus, cannot be sustained. The world is still as dependent upon the productivity of the land, and the people who farm the land, as in the days of hunting and gathering—and will remain so in the future. Sustainability, including the sustainability of human civilization, ultimately will require a return to the traditions and culture of agriculture in creating a sustainable agriculture.

The lack of sustainability to industrial agriculture is not a matter of personal opinion; it is the logical result of scientific reasoning.

The differences between *sustainable* and *industrial* approaches to farming are deep and fundamental. Nothing is more fundamental to a farm, a factory, or an economy than its purpose, and the purposes of industrial and sustainable organizations are very different. The central purpose of an *industrial* organization is *productivity*. Industrial organizations are organized and managed to achieve maximum output with minimum input, which in economic terms translates into maximum profits. Larger industrial organizations, like larger farms, typically are able to produce greater values of output with lower costs of inputs, so organizational growth results in ever-greater profitability and productivity. Thus, the guiding principles of an industrial agriculture are *maximum profits and growth*.

The purpose of all *sustainable* organizations, on the other hand, is *permanence*—sustained productivity. Sustainable organizations, including sustainable farms, must be organized and managed to conserve, renew, and regenerate their resource base, as well as to be productive and profitable. Rather than maximize or minimize, sustainable farmers must manage for balance and harmony among the ecological, social, and economic dimensions of their farms. They must care for the land to preserve its regenerative capacity as well as its productivity. They must care for their customers and neighbors to preserve the society within which, and for which, they exist. All organizations are similarly dependent upon nature and society for their sustainability. Only through caring for nature and caring for people can organizations sustain their productivity, maintain economic viability, and thus achieve their purpose of permanence. The guiding principles of any sustainable organization are *balance and harmony* among *ecological* integrity, *social* responsibility, and *economic* viability.

Sustainability and Usefulness

At first thought, many farmers may see little to be gained from thinking about such abstract concepts as purpose and principles. They are interested in farming, not philosophizing. However, nothing is more critical, not just to the sustainable farming but also to sustainable living. If we fail to pursue permanence through the ecological, social, and economic principles of sustainability, we not only threaten the future of humanity, we threaten our own pursuit of happiness. It isn't just about philosophy; it's about our farms, our families, and our lives.

The lack of sustainability to industrial agriculture is not a matter of personal opinion; it is the logical result of scientific reasoning. The laws of thermodynamics are among the most fundamental laws of science. The first law of thermodynamics states that the total of energy and matter is conserved. Energy may change in form, energy may change into matter, or matter may change into energy, but total energy, including energy embodied in matter, remains unchanged. Thus, sustainability might seem ensured. However, the second law of thermodynamics states that each time energy changes in form, or energy changes into matter or matter to energy, some of the *usefulness* of energy is lost.

This may sound complicated, but it is really fairly simple once you understand that the *usefulness* of energy refers to the capability of energy to perform *work* and is directly related to the *concentration* of energy. Work inevitably dissipates energy, changing it from more- to less-concentrated forms. So when energy becomes less concentrated, as when matter is transformed into energy, it becomes less *useful*. Dissipated energy can be *reused*, but it must be *re-concentrated* and *re-stored* to restore its usefulness. Unfortunately, energy required to concentrate and to store energy is no longer available to do work; its *usefulness* is lost. Scientists refer to this process as a natural tendency toward *entropy*, "the ultimate state reached in degradation of matter and energy; a state of inert uniformity of component elements; absence of form, pattern, hierarchy, or differentiation." A barren desert, without form, structure, or pattern, without life, is about as close to entropy as most of us have seen. Given the natural tendency toward entropy, sustainability might seem impossible.

Sustainability is possible only if *new* energy is made available to offset the energy inevitably lost when energy is used in performing any type of *work*. Without an infusion of new energy, the total supply of useful energy in any system eventually will be depleted. Fortunately, the sun provides solar energy, which is the only source of *new* energy on earth. Thus, systems that fail to utilize same form of solar energy to offset the unavoidable energy lost in performing work inevitably tend toward entropy.

Industrial organizations, including industrial farming operations, are very productive, meaning very efficient in doing *work* because they focus on *extracting* energy and *using* nothing to *re-concentrate, restore, or regenerate energy*, unless such processes improve the efficiency of energy extraction and use. When they deplete one source of energy—meaning either natural or human resources—they simply find new sources. Resource regeneration and renewal are *non-productive* energy uses; it is more efficient to extract and exploit new resources. Once all sources of energy have been depleted, however, energy-extracting systems lose their ability to do *work*; they reach entropy. So an industrial agriculture will eventually lose its ability to produce; it's not a matter of if, but when.

The same scientific concepts apply to *non-material* forms of production, specifically human labor or other personal services. The energy resources in this case are social rather than physical in nature. Social capital or social energy is embodied or stored in the ability of people to benefit from relationships with each other, within families, communities, and societies. Kinships within families, friendships within communities, and civility within societies all contribute directly to our happiness and quality of life but also contribute to our ability to *work* together, to be *productive* and *useful* to each other.

The corporately controlled, global food supply chain is a natural consequence of unbridled economic industrialization as agribusinesses relentlessly pursue ever-greater profits and growth.

Social Entropy

Industrial organizations are very efficient in utilizing human resources because they focus on using existing social relationships to facilitate production. But again, they do nothing to regenerate or restore the social capital that is inevitably lost. In industrial societies, families become business organizations, friendships become business relationships, and citizens become consumers, and little more. The social cohesiveness that makes societies productive as well as personally rewarding is lost. Using *social energy* to establish, maintain, and renew positive social relationships is considered *non-productive* use; it is more efficient to find new people, communities, and societies to exploit. Exploited societies, left without a sense of fairness, equity, or justice inevitably fall into patterns of conflicts, which lead to the destruction of both natural and human resources. The results of depleted social resources may be witnessed in many parts of the world today. An industrial society inevitably tends toward *social entropy.*

Economies simply provide means of facilitating relationships among people and between people and their natural environment in complex societies. There are simply too many people to produce their own food, clothing, and shelter or to barter with each other. Economies actually, *produce* nothing; but they do facilitate production. All economic capital, meaning anything capable of producing economic value, is extracted from either natural capital or social capital. Thus, when all of the natural and social capital in a system has been extracted and exploited, all of the energy in the system has been dissipated, and it can no longer produce anything of economic value; it has reached a state of *economic entropy.*

Industrial farms maximize productivity through specialization and standardization (facilitating routinization, mechanization, and automation), which allows consolidation of management into ever-larger farms.

In addition, industrial systems also diminish the social and personal quality of life of people within society in ways that have nothing to do with individual, material well-being. Nature provides direct benefits to people, through a healthy living environment, clean air and water, aesthetically pleasing landscapes, and opportunities to connect and commune with nature. Society also provides direct benefits to people, through personal relationships within families and communities and through equity and justice within societies. Direct personal relationships among people and between people and nature also help give purpose and meaning to our lives. The quality of our life, our happiness, is directly related to a sense of *rightness* in our relationships with people and nature. This rightness is determined within a higher order of things, which transcends the economy, society, and nature. Within this order, the unrestrained extraction and exploitation violates our common sense of rightness. An industrial agriculture may enhance our material well-being, but it diminishes our social and spiritual happiness and quality of life.

We have created an industrial agriculture economy and it is inevitably trending toward entropy. It is simply not sustainable. It is extractive and exploitative, rather than regenerative and renewing, and it is rapidly running out of energy to extract and people to exploit. The corporately controlled, global food supply chain is a natural consequence of unbridled economic industrialization as agribusinesses relentlessly pursue ever-greater profits and growth. The new biotechnologies and information technologies are nothing but new tools to facilitate the continued unbridled exploitation of the resources and people of the world. Our industrial food system is like a cancerous tumor, multiplying and growing uncontrolled until it ultimately destroys the life of its host, the people it purports to feed. The tumor of industrial economic development, including industrial agriculture, is rapidly depleting the fossil energy upon which it depends for its continued growth and ultimately for its life. If we fail to choose a sustainable alternative to industrialization, human civilization will not survive. . . .

Permanence, Not Maximum Productivity

If we are to develop a sustainable agriculture, we must learn to manage our resources for permanence rather than maximum productivity. Industrial farms maximize productivity through specialization and standardization (facilitating routinization, mechanization, and automation), which allows consolidation of management into ever-larger farms. Industrial farms are inherently mechanistic, operating like sophisticated machines with many interrelated and replaceable parts, each performing a specific specialized function by a predefined standard procedure. This mechanistic way of farming has proved very effective in extracting the fertility of the land and exploiting farm workers, rural people, and even farmers for short-run profits and growth. But, it does nothing to renew the natural productivity of the soil or to regenerate the capacity of farmers or farm workers. It leaves no legacy of productive land and people for the next generation.

A sustainable agriculture, on the other hand, mimics the processes of living, biological systems. Living systems are self-making, self-renewing, reproductive, and regenerative. Living systems have the capacity to capture and store solar energy to offset the energy that is inevitably lost in the processes of re-concentrating and re-storing energy. Obviously, individual living organisms are not permanent or sustainable since all living things eventually die. But, all living things have the capacity to devote part of their productive capacity to regeneration and reproduction, creating new generations of life. Thus, communities of living things are regenerative and thus sustainable. Living human communities also have culture and traditions, which are passed from one generation to the next. All living systems—including farms and communities—are capable of permanence as well as productivity. A sustainable agriculture must utilize these capacities.

Fortunately, much of what we need to do to create new sustainable agricultural and food systems can be found in the culture and traditions of American agriculture. Not that traditional American agriculture was sustainable, because it clearly was not. Even before the era of agrichemicals, farmers mined the natural fertility of their land and allowed its top soil to erode. But, within the traditions of agriculture was a culture that embraced the fundamental principles of sustainability, farmers just didn't understand the consequences of their farming choices. Traditionally, farmers treated their farms as living systems; they cared about the land, cared about their neighbors and customers, not just about themselves. Their lives were connected to past, current, and future generations.

Sustainable farmers choose appropriate technologies, which increase the productive capacities of people rather than replace people with computers and machines.

In the culture of farming, land was a sacred trust—something to be used, but also protected and nurtured, so it could be passed on to the next generation as healthy and productive as when it was passed to this generation from the last. Many farmers didn't really know how to care for the land, but they really did care. Farmers thought of themselves as stewards of earth, taking care of something for the benefit of others, even when they expected no individual benefit. Traditionally, farmers were members of families, of communities, and of society, who realized that they benefited from their predecessors and from their relationships with other people, in ways that had nothing to do with economics.

In traditional farming culture, farmers worked in harmony with nature, nurturing the natural ability of plants and animals to capture and to transform solar energy into foods and fibers of usefulness and of value to people. They didn't always know how to work with nature, but they tried. Traditionally, farmers worked in harmony with their communities and society, trusting that they would be rewarded—economically, socially, and spiritually. They didn't always treat others as we would expect to be treated today, but they felt a responsibility to society. The culture of agriculture was a legacy of both land and people, built upon the legacy handed down from past generations for the benefit of future generations. The traditions and culture of agriculture are very much in harmony with the purpose and principles of sustainability.

Thankfully, it is not too late to choose, but the innovations needed for a sustainable future are more challenging than the industrial innovations of the past. Sustainable farming is management intensive, thinking farming. They are less dependent on non-renewable fossil energy because they rely more on management of their on-farm, renewable resources. Sustainable farmers translate observation into information, information into knowledge, and knowledge into an understanding of how nature works and how to work with it. Sustainable farming is also feeling farming, which translates understanding into the wisdom needed to distinguish right from wrong. Sustainable farmers don't just produce food; they produce ecological and social benefits, both for current and future generations. They care for the land and care about their neighbors and customers. Thus, sustainable farmers must have ethical and social integrity as well as intellect. Sustainable farmers are thinking workers—or working thinkers—as well as thoughtful, caring people. Sustainable farming combines the physical, mental, and spiritual dimensions of productivity, which requires innovation, creativity, knowledge, and wisdom.

A Quantum Leap Forward

Sustainable farming does not mean going back to the drudgery of farming in the past. Sustainable farmers choose appropriate technologies, which increase the productive capacities of people rather than replace people with computers and machines. Admittedly, farming sustainably requires some physical work, but work can be good for the body as well as the mind and soul. Sustainable farming is not a step backward from industrial agriculture; it is a quantum leap forward to something fundamentally better.

Most small farms today are still small because they have rejected the industrial paradigm in favor of more traditional approaches to farming. Some have already joined the sustainable agriculture movement, but to most small farmers, both sustainable and traditional, the values of family and community are still important in their farming decisions. Most small farmers know they can't compete with large corporate operations for global markets, so they don't mine their land and exploit their neighbors in a futile attempt to be the world's most efficient producers. Most small farmers simply have not abandoned the traditions and culture of farming for the sake of profits and growth. Ironically, these small farmers, who have [been] written off as irrelevant, are now well positioned for success in a rapidly changing world.

No one articulates the small farm advantage more eloquently than does [writer] Wendell Berry: "Farming by the measure of nature, which is to say the nature of the particular place, means that farmers must tend farms that they know and love, farms small enough to know and love, using tools and methods they know and love, in the company of neighbors they know and love." And I might add, producing food for people they know and love. A farmer can only truly know and love so much land and so many people, so the most successful farms of the future will be those that are appropriately small.

It is not too late to choose sustainability over entropy. We still have remnants of farming traditions that are consistent with the purpose of permanence and the ecological, social, and economic principles of sustainability. We still have . . . small farmers who are still on the land who are searching for ways to make a good living without abandoning their God-given responsibilities to take care of their land and to care for their neighbors. We have thousands of bright young people who would like to join them, if they just had some help in getting started. We can reject the false promises of an industrial agriculture, which relies on unending extraction and exploitation in a word of dwindling fossil energy and growing social conflict. We can place our confidence and trust in the ability of America's small farmers to be innovative, creative, and thoughtful in their relationships with the land, with their neighbors and customers, and we can reward them adequately for their contributions.

The world is changing for either better or worse. I don't know what a new sustainable food system will look like, but I know it will not be the industrial system of today. Perhaps it will be a *global* network of *local* food systems, linking small independent, farmers with independent food processors and food retailers. I don't know that farms in the future will be small, but I know they will be different from industrial farms today. Farming innovations of the future must link the intellectual capacities of farmers with farming traditions of taking care of the land and caring for people. Innovation through tradition will be the key to small farm success in a changing world.

9

Health-Care Management Can Benefit from Automation

Avi Hoffer

Avi Hoffer is founder and chairman of Metastorm Inc., a provider of business management software, in Baltimore, Maryland.

The complex, burdensome task of health-care management can benefit from automation in several ways. Using automated systems and electronic files to streamline processes and activities in record keeping, human resources, accounting, and finance would free health-care professionals and providers from time-consuming paperwork and allow them to focus on patient care. Furthermore, such systems are needed more than ever as the industry faces staff shortages, particularly in administrative support. It is highly recommended that staff participate in the development of their automated systems to ensure that they are comfortable using these technologies.

Ask senior executives in healthcare IT [information technology] what their challenges are, and the answer invariably resembles what healthcare practitioners would say: achieving consistent, beneficial and predictable outcomes. But unlike practitioners who treat known diseases with proven remedies, IT executives struggle with achieving these outcomes because many IT systems are silo-based, are not process-centric and are not easily adaptable.

Hospitals, integrated delivery networks and individual providers are overly burdened with paper-based processes.

Avi Hoffer, "BPM: Antidote to Inefficiency," *Health Management Technology*, vol. 24, January 2003, pp. 40–43. www.healthmgttech.com/cgi-bin/arttop.asp?Page=h0103 bpm.htm. Copyright © 2003 Nelson Publishing. Reproduced by permission.

They need to comply with documentation requirements in the highly regulated environment as well as handle and track back-office processes for collections, procurement and other functions.

While the patchwork of paper trails and processes gets results, it lacks efficiency and siphons away resources from the primary mission of providing patient care. Also, expectations are higher for improved productivity at every level, from registering patients to purchasing supplies. Using finite resources to balance the need for patient care with the requirements of administration is a constant effort.

HIPAA Sets the Tone

Use of electronic records lowers the burden of managing information, and passage of the Health Insurance Portability and Accountability Act (HIPAA) accelerated the move to electronic records. For the past three years, organizations have improved record-keeping, implemented technology and put the means in place to ensure compliance. With compliance already or soon required for HIPAA components, organizations have now begun to shoulder the ongoing burden of the management of manual processes and reports required by HIPAA.

This added burden comes at a time when the healthcare industry is experiencing staff shortages and movements to limit the working hours of healthcare professionals. With severe shortages in the patient service staff, hiring more administrative support is low on the priority list. Additionally, as HIPAA requirements are not revenue-producing activities, they do not provide the financial return to enable organizations to hire employees devoted to compliance.

New mandates without a corresponding increase in staff require managers to squeeze additional productivity out of an already strapped workforce. Healthcare organizations must rethink the way their employees work—specifically, the way they handle the administrative processes that allow the organization to operate.

This includes processes related to human resources, accounting, finance, personnel and information technology. These underlying processes must be optimized because electronic records are only a reflection of a process and, by themselves, don't offer peak efficiency.

Why Processes?

Processes govern every area of an organization and are key to productivity, but they are often the cause of confusion, too, with many still paper-based and inconsistently applied. A medium- to large-size healthcare organization may have thousands of processes, each with its own form and steps for completion. When there needs to be an exception to a process, the labor required to reconcile it is all manual.

Processes initially arise in organizations to increase productivity. If everyone requesting time off follows the same procedure and uses the same document, it eases the burden on managers who need to approve the requests. The same concept applies to expense reports, personnel changes, performance reviews, purchase orders and time sheets.

At a certain point, the benefits of this standardization begin to falter. Departments are overloaded with paperwork, and employees are confused about which forms to fill out, and how and when to submit them. Confusion and frustration result in a decrease in adherence to established processes. Busy employees find it faster to ignore the forms and skip steps in established processes.

In some cases, disregard for established processes is an inconvenient breach of organizational policy. But in HIPAA-related activities, ignoring processes could result in regulatory penalties and a loss of patient trust.

Treating the Symptoms

Trying to fix the problem of managing an overwhelming amount of paper with a solution that creates electronic records is like prescribing aspirin for an ache: It may help, but it is only fixing one ailment that delivers the most pain.

In healthcare IT, a record usually remains electronic until it needs to be shared with another person, at which time the document is printed and hand-delivered or mailed to the recipient. Once it arrives, data are re-entered by hand into another database or electronic system, and upon completion, the record is often printed out, photocopied, signed and filed—all defeating the purpose of paperless initiatives.

Like the incomplete diagnosis of the patient's pain, making records electronic does not address the fundamental causes of inefficiency. Efficiency comes from a systematic approach to processes, much like an antibiotic would treat a variety of illnesses instead of a point solution like aspirin. Systems must be integrated throughout the organization for a process to offer true efficiency, avoiding duplication or omission of data during entry and re-entry. Storage, also, is more efficient when processes are managed and optimized electronically.

Process Management

A comprehensive solution that addresses the interaction of people and processes, Business Process Management (BPM) is more than eliminating paper or automating the work. BPM is to processes as Six Sigma [a system to eliminate defects] is to manufacturing: It makes organizations focus on what people and pathways are most important to fulfilling a process, how to handle process exceptions with a fail-safe element, what the process can deliver and ensuring consistent, predictable outcomes.

Healthcare organizations have invested heavily in systems that fulfill core functions and comply with HIPAA. But what happens when those systems are presented with an exception or other unpredictable event? For example, if provider reimbursements are delayed because of discrepancies between insurers, how easily do these get processed? In many cases, they are handled manually, which can dramatically slow down cash flow.

BPM technology extends the functionality of these systems by automating the front end of processes, integrating the back-end systems and streamlining the whole activity. With the process handled entirely through the system, progress can be tracked, and compliance with best practices is ensured and proven through a detailed audit trail. The end result is that it lowers the organization's operational costs and tees it up to improve revenue.

It's imperative that healthcare entities leverage appropriate technology solutions.

Process automation and management with BPM goes beyond the limited functionality of commercial, off-the-shelf electronic form applications, and differs from the labor-intensive, machine-to-machine connectivity of traditional integration technologies. BPM incorporates people into processes because, at some point, people are needed to make decisions about data.

Empowerment of staff begins at the "mapping stage" of the technology, where business-level staff create a visual depiction of the process using graphical BPM tools. The mapping stage introduces staff to a new way of thinking about how they approach work instead of merely how to get the job done. It makes them ask questions like, "Who needs to be part of this process, what do they need, and who or what ensures that the process is followed, not simply rubber-stamped?"

The process of involving staff in the creation stage accomplishes two goals. First, staff design the process in the way that makes sense to them, so it is likely to be accepted. Second, the development team is greatly expanded. Rather than assigning the IT team to design and automate thousands of processes, this distributed approach lets the users design the process and the developers implement it. The end result is a more rapid deployment of automated processes because the implementation work has been distributed throughout the organization.

The technology creates a road map for users to manage their processes effectively in an electronic environment. Staff immediately see opportunities to improve efficiency, such as the bottlenecks that can occur if some individuals are unnecessarily included in a review process. Staff also find that some processes may be eliminated altogether because they are duplicated elsewhere.

Once a process is implemented, changes are made quickly through the process map, avoiding the need for organization-wide memos announcing policy chances. Because the routing system can be role-based rather than individual-based, personnel changes have no impact on the processes.

Expanding Efficiency

By automating the work and the flow between stations, employees do not need to learn the minutia of regulation compliance. They perform tasks assigned to them, and the system handles the procedure. Negligent or intentional violations of procedure are not possible. This eases the burden of regulatory changes on employees and eliminates the possibility of accidental violations.

By automating processes from beginning to end, process participants see the status of the item on their individual desktops, and automated alerts notify management if compliance is slow or nonexistent. Through automation, users get the personalized information they need to make a decision and complete their step in the process, and digital signatures and other verification methods ensure the integrity of the information. BPM removes excuses for not following proper procedures.

The healthcare industry relies upon adherence to established practices and structured activities to ensure that medical staff can address the needs of patients. That level of efficiency needs to be expanded throughout the organization so that operational activity supports the medical mission. This means more than just using less paper or use of electronic records; it means following processes that result in consistent, beneficial and predictable outcomes.

These processes will continue to evolve due to government mandates such as HIPAA and industry regulations. As such, it's imperative that healthcare entities leverage appropriate technology solutions, not only to maintain flexibility to modify processes but also to extend existing systems and to allow for fast exception processing. That's predictability.

10

Health-Care Management May Not Benefit from Automation

Barry Chaiken

Barry Chaiken is associate chief medical officer of BearingPoint, a technology and management consulting firm based in Texas.

Automating the management of medical records, medication, and other administrative and clerical systems in health care may not be living up to its promises of increased productivity, accuracy, and cost-effectiveness. Health-care providers are slow to adopt these expensive new technologies. Additionally, a recent study shows that one medication administration system was error-prone, poorly designed, and incompatible with existing systems. In order for health-care management automation to be truly efficient, information technology and medical professionals must work closely to revamp these systems.

After a brief reprieve during the 1990s, healthcare again faces the vexing problem of rising healthcare costs with accompanying increases in premiums and out-of-pocket costs for consumers—who are expecting better outcomes.

For some time now clinical information technology [IT] has been seen as the solution. Increasing numbers of organizations invest millions of dollars in clinical systems such as computerized physician order entry (CPOE), electronic medical records, clinician portals, wireless networks and medication administration systems.

Barry Chaiken, "Innovative Health Care Takes More than Just IT Automation," *Wisconsin Technology Network*, May 18, 2005. http://wistechnology.com/article.php?id=1838. Reproduced by permission.

Although some anecdotal reports have proved these new solutions to be promising, others have reported on delayed implementations, low clinician adoption and the delivery of poorer outcomes.

While the failure to implement a CPOE system at Cedars-Sinai Medical Center in Los Angeles a few years back has been widely publicized, additional failed or lagging clinical IT implementations are not uncommon. Many clinical IT vendors report privately about their struggles to get systems up and running. What is surprising is the recently reported evidence of clinical IT delivering increased medical errors, a result intuitively not expected, and for many, quite disappointing.

In a study published in the *Journal of the American Medical Association*, [sociologist Ross] Koppel, et al. reported how a CPOE system installed at an academic medical institution facilitated medication errors. The authors attributed many of the 22 types of errors to a variety of factors, including poor system design coupled with incompatible care delivery processes. These results highlight the importance of processes in the delivery of expected outcomes.

It is well known that the application of best practices and evidence-based medicine (EBM) can significantly improve clinical and financial outcomes. Many informatics experts have long thought that the implementation of clinical IT systems would bring these best practices more effectively to the physician, thereby reducing unnecessary variation in care, accelerating the adoption of new, proven diagnostic and therapeutic approaches, and decreasing costs associated with ineffectual or inappropriate care. What we are finding is that the results delivered by this new technology are falling far short of their promise.

The failure of these clinical IT tools to deliver safer, more efficient care is due to many factors, yet all of them have origin in the concept inherent in the phrase "path innovation."

Although the theories and expertise that form the basis of path innovation are not new, their interaction with and subsequent impact on clinical IT is.

To implement and effectively leverage clinical IT systems, a new approach in the use of experts is required. Path innovation integrates different subject-matter experts in unique ways to leverage their expertise throughout the design and implementation of clinical IT systems. Even for systems already built, path innovation can be used to better leverage existing functionality in these clinical IT systems. It can help enhance outcomes while reducing the probability of unacceptable results such as system-related medical and medication errors.

Three Keys to Path Innovation

Path innovation depends on three key factors: (1) process improvement or re-engineering, (2) clinical guidelines, clinical paths and evidence-based medicine, and (3) IT system design. Although subject-matter experts exist in all these areas, it is unclear how well these experts historically worked together in the design and implementation of clinical IT systems.

- Process improvement experts understand how processes impact outcomes and what analytical steps are needed to evaluate processes. They are able to suggest changes in processes and predict the potential improvements such changes will deliver.

They often appear on the scene late in implementations if at all. Working within the environment as presented to them, they try to change existing processes without the advantage of being able to change the inputs (e.g., clinical path) or tools (e.g., clinical IT system and its functionality) of the processes.

- Experts in clinical content understand what various clinical paths deliver as outcomes. They are able to link various interventions with probabilistic results.

Clinical content experts develop clinical content focused solely on clinical issues, rarely incorporating IT system design or clinical process considerations in their work. This is evident in the effort invested by many organizations to modify existing guidelines to fit their newly implemented clinical IT systems. Their reported struggles are indicative of the difficulty of this type of work.

- Designers of IT systems understand the flow of digital information within computer systems and the user interfaces that receive and deliver data to users. They are able to conceptualize how a data point can be stored or reformatted with other data points.

Almost universally, these experts work and apply their expertise independently of each other. IT system designers develop clinical IT systems using specifications developed by product managers who attempt to bridge IT with healthcare. These product managers are rarely experts in clinical medicine or clinical processes.

Form a Path Innovation Team

Path innovation requires the formation of a team of subject-matter experts that apply their skills during an entire clinical IT system project. During the system design phase, clinical and process design experts share their understanding of their discipline with the IT system developer.

During the implementation phase, the IT system designer and the clinical content expert act as consultants to the process redesigner to develop new processes that are both radically different from existing processes and that could only be implemented utilizing functionality made available by the new clinical IT system. In addition, the clinical content expert can use this functionality to conceive of clinical paths impossible without this digital healthcare capability.

Although path innovation builds upon existing approaches, it reflects a new way of thinking and approaching problems. Instead of looking at how an existing process could be modified, path innovation requires the birth of brand new processes formerly impossible in the institution before the installation of the new clinical IT system. To accomplish this, organizations need to identify subject-matter experts who are also able to achieve a basic understanding of the disciplines of their expert colleagues. Then together, these experts work to create new processes that incorporate the needs of the institution with the promise of new IT systems and clinical content.

An expert in clinical processes once said, "[E]very system is perfectly designed to achieve exactly the results it gets." Assuming this to be true, only through the creation of truly new systems (e.g., processes) using path innovation can we expect to impact results to achieve the safer and higher-quality healthcare that we all desire.

11

Smart Homes Can Assist the Lives of the Elderly

Institute for the Future

The Institute for the Future (IFTF) is an independent nonprofit research group that specializes in technological, business, and social trends.

Smart homes, in which automation and other technologies assist with household tasks and chores, and monitor the home and its residents, offer the elderly great benefits. Smart homes are a superior alternative to nursing homes; they are cost-effective and can allow the elderly to live independently and be happier. Smart homes also can help the elderly to keep in touch with and be closely supervised by other family members, and to follow daily routines such as taking medications. As the population ages in industrialized nations, the elderly will adopt smart homes and assistive technologies to remain self-reliant.

There will be a wide variety of smart homes, each configured to meet the needs and interests of its residents. People who are interested in shrinking their energy budgets may never be in the market for a virtual butler, and *vice versa.*

Instead, people will be likely to create "hotspots" of intelligent appliances in specific rooms, to serve particular purposes. One family may focus on home-entertainment-system networking; their neighbors may prefer appliances to manage household tasks; while their elderly parents may want tech-

Institute for the Future, "Smart Homes & Social Devices: RFID Takes Off," *The Futures of RFID: A Memo Series*, Palo Alto, CA: Institute for the Future, 2005. © 2005 Institute for the Future. All rights reserved. Reproduced by permission.

nologies to help them stay healthy. Few homeowners will invest in systems that make their entire home "smart."

Recent research suggests that there will be no single configuration defining the smart home of the future. There will be many different designs, which mix and match a variety of technologies to perform a multitude of tasks.

Elders Will Be Early and Important Adopters

Elders will have good reason to adopt intelligent appliances. A remote control for your house is an expensive, cool toy. A system that enables an 80-year old woman to continue to live safely in her own home, while advising her children whether she's okay or has become ill or depressed, offers life-changing benefits.

Technologies that allow elders to "age-in-place" look even more appealing once you consider the high cost—both financial and psychological—of nursing homes, let alone weighing the projected shortage of nurses throughout the rapidly aging, advanced world.

Elders won't just be early adopters, they will become influencers. Aging-in-place technologies will have powerful multiplier effects. Unlike smart kitchens or house remote controls, assisted-living technologies deliver benefits to entire families. Some systems, like the Digital Family Portrait, will help keep elders and their families connected. Others will provide regular updates about an elder's condition to physicians and/or family members. Finally, all aging-in-place technologies will allow families to avoid—or at least delay—the upheaval of moving elders out of their homes.

Variety of Intelligent Appliances

There are a variety of intelligent-appliance technologies; each designed to serve different markets and functions.

Convenience Systems Today, you can buy systems that are essentially remote controls for your whole house. These provide centralized displays that allow you to program the dishwasher from your bathroom or turn on the home theater system from your kitchen. Marketing of these devices has been aimed at wealthy, tech-savvy homeowners. While they will continue to have a place in high-end homes, such devices are not likely to reach the mass market. It is more likely that some other common home electronic equipment—TV cable box or personal computer, for example—will take on some of the functionality provided by these centralized systems.

Infrastructure Control Infrastructure systems—which are largely still under development—manage heating and cooling, turn lights off and on depending upon room occupancy, and schedule household tasks for off-peak hours. These systems are designed to reduce energy and water consumption.

Other systems aim to be more like software agents for the kitchen, helping you prepare a meal from the seemingly random contents of your refrigerator, sending a shopping list to the online grocer, and suggesting menu options for a weekend dinner party.

Each system will continue to have its advocates. But the coming global wave of elders will demand other kinds of intelligent appliances: technologies that help them stay connected to family, friends, and caregivers, and technologies that help them manage everyday tasks and remain in control of their homes and their lives.

Maintenance and Complexity Management Many "smart appliances" are designed to simplify household management. Prototype smart refrigerators that "know" their contents, suggest dinner menus, and can order groceries online, offer the prospect of reducing the complexity of routine tasks. As do prototype smart washing machines that read RFID [radio frequency identification] tags on garments and warn users of mismatched items or tailor wash cycles.

Many intelligent appliances will be variations of current prototypes, with one key difference. They will be smart through connectivity to other devices or software and will use common data interchange standards (like [markup language] XML) to share and act on information. The smart refrigerator of the future is more likely to create menu recommendations by gathering information from both the household schedule database and a medical software agent that tracks food allergies and nutriceutical prescriptions than to contain all that information, itself. Smart washing machines will consult schedules and weather forecasts to see what clothes will be needed and when they need to be cleaned.

Another important category of RFID-enabled intelligent appliances will be "gateway devices." which monitor the passage of RFID tags. For example, a system that helps families keep track of everything they needed to take with them would consist of a database and an RFID reader installed in a doorway. The reader might be programmed to always check for particular items, like car keys, backpacks, or lunch boxes. If the middleware could talk to a family scheduling program (say, Mom's PDA [personal digital assistant]), it could perform more detailed, time-specific checks.

Such a system would not require cheap tags to be useful, for two reasons. First, items like purses and backpacks are large enough to carry larger, more expensive tags; other items, like a child's house key or a parent's cell phone, may be less expensive, but still worth tracking because of the inconvenience caused by not having them.

The Coming Global Wave of Elders

Today's intelligent appliances are aimed at wealthy early adopters. But the future of these appliances lies with the rapidly growing number of elderly in North America, Europe, and

Asia. As many companies now realize, retiring baby boomers are going to constitute an important new market in the coming years. Indeed, the aging of the boomers is a symptom of a broader aging of advanced societies. In the United States, the share of the population over age 65 will increase from 13% in 2000 to 20% by 2050.

Aging Is a Global Phenomenon While the aging of baby boomers has received plenty of attention in the American press, it is a global phenomenon. The share of elderly in Europe and Asia (and to a lesser degree, in Latin America) will also rise.

Some of the world's most advanced national markets are also its fastest-aging. Japan, for example, has one of the highest proportions of elderly in the world. Nearly 20% of the population is over 60 years old. At the same time, birth rates in Japan are falling—meaning that there are fewer young workers to care for the old. Forty percent of Japan's elderly are over the age of 75, and that share will reach 48% by the year 2020. A growing number of elders are living alone: about 15% live independently now, a figure that will grow to about 25% by the year 2020. As Japanese economist Naohira Ogawa noted, "Compared to the United States, it is nothing." But given that multigenerational households have been the norm, the fact that more elders are living alone represents "a major revolution as far as Japan is concerned." Korea faces a similar situation; by 2020 the elderly will make up 15% of the population (some 7 million in all) and life expectancy will also rise.

Generation of Elders Will Redefine Old Age This generation will redefine old age, work hard to remain active and independent, and possess the financial means to support such efforts.

The boomer generation has been a global cultural force and center of market attention since the 1960s. Its members are used to having their tastes reflected in the market and will not accept the public marginalization and personal frailty that has defined age in the past. As Harvard public health professor Jay Winsten put it, "boomers won't stand for being put out to pasture."

Aging boomers will be too attractive of a market to ignore. In developed countries, people over age 50 own three-quarters of all financial assets and half of all discretionary spending power. They have more time to spend their money. A few decades ago, most people lived only a few years beyond retirement. In contrast, workers retiring today can look forward to 15–30 years of leisure. Thanks to medical advances and healthier living, they can also expect to remain active longer.

Free time, health, and relative financial comfort are creating a mature market of immense potential. Over the last two decades, consumption by the over-50s in Europe has increased three times as fast as that by the rest of the population. In industrialized countries, people over 50 buy about half of all new cars (a fact of which auto makers are just starting to respond).

Aging in Place and Intelligent Appliances

How will elders cope with the challenges of aging? Many will turn to connective and assistive technologies to remain independent and continue living in their homes. The former will help elders remain active, and the latter will help them with daily tasks that they can no longer complete themselves.

Connective systems keep active, independent elders in touch with family and friends.

The ideal smart house used to be thought of as one that would take care of everything for you. It would be a "machine for living in," to borrow modern architect Le Courbusier's phrase. In contrast, some of today's best scientists aim to create systems that help residents do things, instead of systems that do things for them. As professor Stephen Intille has described the MIT [Massachusetts Institute of Technology] House_n project:

> Our primary vision is not one where computer technology ubiquitously and proactively manages the details of the home. Technology should require human effort in ways that keep life as mentally and physically challenging as possible as people age.

Work on communications and monitoring systems has taken off thanks, in part, to the discovery of a clear relationship between isolation and depression. Elders are much more likely to stay active when their social lives are active and they're in touch with family and friends. Active elders are healthier elders. Sedentary elders are at greater risk of heart disease, diabetes, and obesity. (Elders often need encouragement to remain active. In Japan and the United States, the elderly watch 5–6 hours of television per day.) Likewise, there is evidence that, by remaining mentally and physically active, elders can fight the onset of Alzheimer's. Having a house that does too much to take care of you, can be bad for you.

More complex assistive systems are designed to help elders who have problems with household tasks or memory.

These insights have driven work on intelligent appliances in two directions: toward the development of connective systems and assistive systems.

Connective Systems Connective systems keep active, independent elders in touch with family and friends. These systems might, for example, remind a user that they haven't talked with a relative in a few days (or, for more distant relatives, in weeks). This system might link with calendaring systems to schedule a get-together with neighbors. They might analyze a resident's sleep and activity patterns, alerting a child or doctor if an elderly parent's routine shifts dramatically—an indication that something could be wrong.

For example, the Digital Family Portrait, developed by Georgia Tech engineers, "reconnects family members by providing a qualitative sense of a distant relative's well-being, while striking a reasonable balance between privacy and the need for information." The portrait's "digital frame changes daily, reflecting a portion of the person's life," and providing a sense of that person's condition.

Assistive Systems Assistive systems are designed to help users with everyday tasks. One early example is the smart medicine chest: cabinets with RFID readers, connected to medical databases and other services. A smart medicine chest would be a delivery platform for a variety of health services. A smart medicine chest could remind users to take their medicine and verify that they've completed a prescription-drug course. It could warn patients against taking drug combinations that produce adverse effects. If connected to a physician's office, the chest could order automatic refills when a prescription runs low.

None of these sounds like a major problem, but they are. Forty percent of prescription-drug courses aren't finished, which keeps people from getting well, helps create new drug-resistant illnesses, and increases overall health care costs. Thousands of people in the United States die each year from adverse drug events caused by unsafe combinations of drugs.

More complex assistive systems are designed to help elders who have problems with household tasks or memory. These consist of monitoring devices in rooms or furniture that closely follow vital signs, provide guidance in preparing meals and other daily tasks, and warn against potential dangers— unattended pot boiling, bath water that's too hot, or clutter on the floor that creates a hazard.

For example, Georgia Tech's Memory Mirror uses RFID tags to sense when an object has been moved and places a photograph of the object on a digital "mirror" showing the last 24 hours. The mirror helps users remember whether they've done daily tasks like feeding pets or taking medicine.

More ambitious is Intel's effort to use wireless sensor networks and embedded computing to assist elderly users compensate for memory impairment. Its CareNet "detects, monitors, and records the daily living activities of an elder by collecting data through postage stamp–sized wireless RFID tags affixed to household objects. Ultimately, the system could help manage everyday activities so that the elders' independence is maintained while relieving some of the burden of around-the-clock care by caregivers."

12

Smart Homes Should Help the Elderly Be Physically and Mentally Active

Stephen S. Intille

Stephen S. Intille is a research scientist and technology director of the House_n Consortium in the Massachusetts Institute of Technology (MIT) Department of Architecture.

Research and development in automation for performing every-day tasks, using appliances, and maintaining the home largely aim to eliminate effort and thinking. However, smart homes and related technologies should be designed to keep the elderly physically and mentally active, providing them with the information to act rather than limiting their sense of control over their surroundings. For instance, wearable devices can assist elderly people with doing chores by guiding their posture and bodily movements. It is also essential that home automation technologies be developed and tested in settings that simulate real-life, long-term scenarios, effort, and learning.

If we are able to believe many movies, television shows, science fiction books, and popular press articles that mention technology and home life in the future, automated systems will replace many routine everyday tasks. In fact, our homes will be so fully automated and "smart" that we will rarely have to think about everyday tasks at all. We will spend nearly all

Stephen S. Intille, "The Goal: Smart People, Not Smart Homes," *Proceedings of the International Conference on Smart Homes and Health Telematics,* Amsterdam: IOS Press, 2006. http://web.media.mit.edu/~intille/papers-files/IntilleICOST06.pdf. Copyright © 2006 reproduced with permission from IOS Press.

of our time in the home engaged in leisure activities, because digital and robotic agents will have taken over the mundane chores of day-to-day life. Researchers and technologists are more cautious in predicting the future of the home. Nevertheless, a survey of ongoing work shows that there is a bias in research toward creating automatic home environments that eliminate the need to think about tasks such as controlling heating and lighting, going to the grocery store, scheduling home appliances, and cooking.

Although the use of automation to help people accomplish tasks they cannot perform on their own because of a disability or frailty may be appropriate in some circumstances, the MIT [Massachusetts Institute of Technology] House_n group argues for a different motivating approach. Rather than striving to create computer technology that ubiquitously and proactively manages the details of the home, perhaps researchers should aim to create technology that *requires* human effort in ways that keep life mentally and physically stimulating as people age. My research group is building and pilot testing novel health systems that use novel ubiquitous computing sensing capabilities to do just that.

The MIT House_n group is working towards a vision where computer technology is ever-present, but in a more subtle way than often advocated in popular culture and even in engineering paper motivation sections. We anticipate that emerging computing systems will use sensors to determine when and how to present information to people at the time and place they need it. We want sensor-driven pervasive technologies to empower people with information that helps them make decisions, but we do not want to strip people of their sense of control over their environment. Losing a sense of control has been shown to be psychologically and physically debilitating. There are technical and human-computer interface advantages of creating systems that attempt to *empower users with information* at "teachable moments" rather than automating much decision making using "smart" or "intelligent" control.

There are technical and human-computer interface advantages of creating systems that attempt to empower users with information at "teachable moments" rather than automating much decision making.

Empowering with Just-in-Time Information

Two ubiquitous computing trends are converging to create a new preventive healthcare opportunity. The first is the rapid adoption of powerful mobile computing devices. The second is the emergence of real-time, context-aware computing. A context-aware computer system can infer what a person is doing from sensor data. For example, two or more accelerometers worn on the body can be used to infer posture, ambulation, and various household activities that involve physical activity (e.g., scrubbing, vacuuming). Soon, these activity detection algorithms will run on mobile phones and acquire sensor data from wearable wireless accelerometers attached to objects worn or carried such as watches or key chains. Sensors placed in the home may allow other everyday activities (e.g., cooking) to be automatically detected as well.

These two trends will enable a new class of just-in-time persuasive interfaces to be created that motivate behavior change by providing well-timed information to users at points of decision, behavior, or consequence. The user's activity inferred from data sensed by mobile devices, can be used to trigger the presentation of messages. Researchers in health behavior fields have convincingly demonstrated the power of point-of-decision messaging to motivate behavior change.

A review of the preventive health prompting literature suggests that there are five components to an effective strategy to motivate behavior change using just-in-time information: 1) present a simple, tailored message that is easy to understand, 2) at an appropriate time, 3) at an appropriate place, 4) using a nonirritating, engaging, and tailored strategy, 5) repeatedly and consistently. Context detection algorithms provide information that can trigger messages at an appropriate time, and mobile computers allow message presentation at the appropriate place. Mobile computers are also becoming personal archiving devices, recording sensor data about user experience, such as where the user goes and what the user does. These databases can therefore be exploited to tailor feedback to a person in engaging ways based upon past experiences and the current context. Prompts that are not only timely but also tailored to the individual are known to be most effective at motivating behavior change. Presenting information repeatedly and consistently (but in a nonirritating way) may be the greatest ubiquitous computing challenge. One way to minimize the likelihood of a message becoming annoying is to ensure that each message has a high perceived value for the user and that it does not appear to be judgmental. This is a challenging design goal because the tendency when developing computer systems that motivate behavior change is to gravitate toward solutions that present messages to the user telling him or her what to do and when (i.e., trying to control rather than subtly inform). Fortunately, sensing technology makes it possible to exploit subtle positive feedback in novel ways. These strategies, however, have yet to be extensively tested outside of traditional labs.

The PlaceLab: A Live-In Laboratory

Designing with a goal of creating systems that teach rather than control impacts both the type of technology that one might design and use as well as the type of evaluation tools that are required to measure success. We need, for example, home environments that allow researchers to measure not only the low-level functioning of technology but also human factors such as whether people are applying what they learn, whether they are receptive to information presented by technology, and whether the technology is naturally and appropriately integrating information presentation into everyday life activities.

In short, we need the ability to study people using prototype technology in realistic, non-laboratory settings for long periods of time and then measure whether our interventions lead to learning and behavior change. We need good *in situ* [in place] hypothesis-generation tools to ensure that assumptions we make about behavior in the lab hold true in more realistic (and complex) situations in real homes.

To address this need, we have designed a single-family home called the PlaceLab with an integrated and ubiquitous sensor architecture. We do not think of this facility as a "smart" or "intelligent" home but instead as a live-in laboratory for researchers to study behavior and technologies. Ubiquitous computing researchers are increasingly turning to sensor-enabled "living laboratories" for the study of people and technologies in settings more natural than a typical laboratory. Volunteer (nonresearcher) participants individually live in the PlaceLab for days or weeks at a time, treating it as a temporary home. Meanwhile, sensing devices integrated into the fabric of the architecture record a detailed description of their activities. The facility generates sensor and observational datasets that can be used for research in ubiquitous computing and other fields where domestic context impacts behavior. We are using the facility to pilot test sensor-driven health applications for motivating (but *not* controlling!) health-related behavior.

Organizations to Contact

The editors have compiled the following list of organizations concerned with the issues debated in this book. The descriptions are derived from materials provided by the organizations. All have publications or information available for interested readers. The list was compiled on the date of publication of the present volume; the information provided here may change. Be aware that many organizations take several weeks or longer to respond to inquiries, so allow as much time as possible.

American Society of Mechanical Engineers (ASME)
Three Park Ave., New York, NY   10016-5990
(800) 843-2763
e-mail: infocentral@asme.org
Web site: www.asme.org

Founded in 1880, ASME is a 120,000-member professional organization focused on technical, educational, and research issues of the engineering and technology community. ASME conducts one of the world's largest technical publishing operations, holds numerous technical conferences worldwide, and offers hundreds of professional development courses each year. It publishes the magazine, *Mechanical Engineering.*

Food and Society (W.K. Kellogg Foundation)
One Michigan Ave. East, Battle Creek, MI   49017-4012
(269) 968-1611 • fax: (269) 968-0413
Web site: www.wkkf.org

Launched in 2000, Food and Society was established by the W.K. Kellogg Foundation, a charitable division of the Kellogg Company. Food and Society is based on a vision of a future food system that (1) provides all segments of society a safe and nutritious food supply, grown in a way that protects health and the environment, and (2) adds economic and social value to rural and urban communities.

House_n Consortium
One Cambridge Center, 4th Floor, Cambridge, MA 02142-1605
e-mail: housen-web@mit.edu
Web site: http://architecture.mit.edu/house_n

House_n is a research group established by the Department of Architecture at the Massachusetts Institute of Technology. It explores ways in which new technologies, materials, and strategies for design can make possible dynamic, evolving places that respond to the complexities of life. Major House_n projects include the PlaceLab and the Open Source Building Alliance.

The Human Factors and Ergonomics Society (HFES)
PO Box 1369, Santa Monica, CA 90406-1369
(310) 394-1811 • fax: 394-2410
e-mail: info@hfes.rog
Web site: www.hfes.org

Founded in 1957, HFES is an interdisciplinary nonprofit organization of psychologists, scientists, engineers, and designers involved in the human factors field. HFES is dedicated to designing systems and devices that are safe and effective for the people who use and maintain them. It publishes several periodicals, including *Human Factors, Ergonomics in Design,* and *HFES Bulletin.*

IEEE Robotics and Automation Society (IEE-RAS), IEEE Corporate Office
3 Park Ave., 17th Floor, New York, NY 10016-5997
(212) 419 7900 • fax: (212) 752 4929
Web site: www.ieee-ras.org

Part of the Institute of Electrical and Electronics Engineers (IEEE), IEEE-RAS is interested in both applied and theoretical issues in robotics and automation. Robotics includes intelligent machines and systems used in space exploration, human services, and manufacturing. Automation involves the use of automated methods in various applications, such as factories, offices, homes, laboratories, and transportation systems, to improve performance and productivity.

Institute for the Future (IFTF)
124 University Ave., 2nd Floor, Palo Alto, CA 94301
(650) 854-6322 • fax: (650) 854-7850
e-mail: info@iftf.org
Web site: www.iftf.org

IFTF is an independent nonprofit research group that specializes in technological, business, and social trends. It is based in California's Silicon Valley and was founded in 1968 by a group of former RAND Corporation researchers with a grant from the Ford Foundation. Copies of the institute's research reports are available free of charge on its Web site.

Instrumentation, Systems, and Automation Society (ISA)
67 Alexander Dr., Research Triangle Park, NC 27709
(919) 549-8411 • fax (919) 549-8288
e-mail: info@isa.org
Web site: www.isa.org

Founded as the Instrument Society of America in 1945, ISA is a global nonprofit organization made up of thirty thousand members worldwide who help each other and other professionals solve difficult technical problems while enhancing their leadership and personal career capabilities. ISA's mission is to develop standards, certify industry professionals, provide education and training, and publish books and articles. ISA hosts the largest conference and exhibition for automation professionals in the Western Hemisphere.

Robotics Industries Association (RIA)
900 Victors Way, Suite 140, Ann Arbor, MI 48106
(734) 994-6088 • fax: (734) 994-3338
Web site: www.roboticsonline.com

Founded in 1974, RIA is North America's only trade association that focuses exclusively on robotics. More than 250 of its member companies represent leading robot manufacturers, system integrators, end users, and researchers. RIA provides robotics news and information on its Web site, Robotics Online.

Bibliography

Books

Rick Baldoz, Charles Koeber, and Philip Kraft, eds.	*The Critical Study of Work: Labor, Technology, and Global Production.* Philadelphia: Temple University Press, 2001.
George A. Bekey	*Autonomous Robots: From Biological Inspiration to Implementation and Control.* Cambridge, MA: MIT Press, 2005.
Beno Benhabib	*Manufacturing: Design, Production, Automation and Integration.* New York: Marcel Dekker, 2003.
Danny Briere and Pat Hurley	*Smart Homes for Dummies.* 3rd Ed. Indianapolis: Wiley, 2007.
Joseph L. Jones	*Robot Programming: A Practical Guide to Behavior-Based Robotics.* New York: McGraw-Hill, 2004.
Jim Pinto	*Automation Unplugged: Pinto's Perspectives, Pointers, & Prognostications.* Research Triangle Park, NC: ISA, 2004.
Jeremy Rifkin	*The End of Work: The Decline of the Global Labor Force and the Dawn of the Post-Market Era.* New York: Jeremy P. Tarcher/Penguin, 2004.

Thomas B. Sheridan	*Humans and Automation: System Design and Research Issues.* Hoboken, NJ: John Wiley & Sons, 2002.
Jon Stenerson	*Industrial Automation and Process Control.* Upper Saddle River, NJ: Prentice Hall, 2003.
Edwin Wise	*Robotics Demystified.* New York: McGraw-Hill, 2005.

Periodicals

Trudy E. Bell	"Getting Automation Some Respect," *The Institute*, March 2007.
Jeremy Caplan	"Cause of Death: Sloppy Doctors," *Time*, January 15, 2007.
Monica Elliott	"Mechanical Logic: Smart Machines Are Getting a Lot of Attention from Engineers and Researchers, but Will They Really Be Able to Think for Themselves?" *Industrial Engineer*, July 1, 2005.
Henrik Eriksson and Toomas Timpka	"The Potential of Smart Homes for Injury Prevention Among the Elderly," *International Journal of Injury Control and Safety Promotion*, June 2002.
Scott Feshuck	"Ladies and Gents, I Present You: The Apocalypse," *Maclean's*, June 11, 2007.

Joel Greenberg "Robotic Cars Could Take Pressure Off Nation's Highways," *Los Angeles Times*, June 23, 2007.

Gregory M. Lamb "Coming Soon: Robo-Greeter," *Christian Science Monitor*, August 30, 2004.

Scott LaFee "A Bot's Life," *San Diego Union-Tribune*, July 12, 2007.

Julia Malone "Farmers, Inventors Explore Automation as Answer to Labor Shortage," *Washington Bureau*, June 1, 2006.

Ted Needleman "Yeah, Sure: The 'Almost' Paperless Office," *Non-Profit Times*, March 1, 2005.

Jim Pinto "Staying Competitive," *Automation World*, July 2007.

Susan K. Schmeichel "Smart Homes Could Up Seniors' Quality of Life," *Pittsburgh Tribune-Review*, October 7, 2002.

Matt Sedensky "Professor Believes Software Can Determine Quality Work," *USA Today*, May 5, 2005.

Margaret Wertheim "Robots That Build (but Still Won't Do Windows)," *New York Times*, March 11, 2004.

Ben Worthen "When Good Call-Center Automation Goes Bad," *Wall Street Journal*, July 11, 2007.

Index

D

Decision aids, 14–15
Department of Defense, 7
Deveol, George, 35
Diamond cartel, 20
Dickey, Bob, 60
Digital Family Portrait, 92, 98
Digital music, 17
Distance learning, 45
Distributed control systems (DCSs), 19

E

Economic entropy, 72
Economy
    automation benefits the, 34–42
    knowledge, 45, 47
Educational system, 47–49
Efficiency, 84–85
Elderly
    growing number of, 95
    smart homes can assist, 91–104
Electric motors, 11–12
Electricity, 60–62
Electronics, in agriculture, 60–62, 66
Empowerment, 101–102
Energy, usefulness of, 70–71
Engelberger, Joseph, 34
Espionage, Soviet, 7
Evidence-based medicine, 87
Expert systems, 14–15

F

Farm workers, 58–59, 66
Farming. See Agriculture
Fast food restaurants
    jobs in, 47

kiosks in, 21–22
replacement of human workers in, 30
Feedback control, 12
Ferguson, Harry S., 59–60
Food engineering, 62
Ford, Henry, 55, 60
Fordson tractor, 55–56
Foreign labor, 42

G

Gateway devices, 94
General Motors, 35–36
Gilder, George, 17
Graafstra, Amal, 8
Great Depression, 31

H

Harvesting equipment, 57–58, 62
Health Insurance Portability and Accountability Act (HIPAA), 80–81
Health-care management
    can benefit from automation, 79–85
    may not benefit from automation, 86–90
Hoffer, Avi, 79
Home automation. See Smart homes
Hotel jobs, 30
House_n project, 97, 101–102
Household management appliances, 93–94
Humanoid robots, as replacement workers, 23–26, 29–33
Humans
    critical issues with automation and, 13–15
    replacement of, with robots, 23–26, 29–33, 43–49